Recycled Container Arts and Crafts Activities

Week-by-Week Projects Using All Kinds of Containers

by Jo Jo Cavalline and Jo Anne O'Donnell

illustrated by Veronica Terrill

Teaching & Learning Company

1204 Buchanan St., P.O. Box 10
Carthage, IL 62321

P9-AQD-372

This book is dedicated to our first and our best teachers, our dads.

Cover photo by Images and More Photography

Copyright © 1996, Teaching & Learning Company

ISBN No. 1-57310-040-4

Printing No. 987654321

Teaching & Learning Company
1204 Buchanan St., P.O. Box 10
Carthage, IL 62321

This book belongs to

Julie Shields

Table of Contents

February

March

April

May

Summer

General

Dear Teacher or Parent,

Don't trash it . . . stash it! Every day our society dumps millions of useable containers into garbage bags and trash cans. As instructors we need to educate our students about the importance of recycling.

Since you are reading this book, we can assume you are an interested person looking for new and innovative ideas for your classroom. Our book will guide you through an organized year of enterprising ideas. We have compiled projects that will enhance your curriculum week by week—from the very beginning in August, right up to take-home summer projects. And we've included a section of special event items such as birthdays, greetings and congratulations. We have incorporated lesson suggestions for various subject areas as well as related literature references into these projects. Each week brings a fresh idea. Each month, we have included a "Read-Treat" for reading motivation. Our "Tips and Suggestions" pages add many other ideas for recycled containers that can be used anytime you feel the need for something new.

So start collecting those containers now! A well-stocked recycling center can be as creative as an overstocked art supply room. Get everyone involved in collecting, but stress the cleanliness and safety aspects of any donations. Many detergents are available in an antibacterial form; look for them and use them in your classroom and on your supplies. Sharp edges, small pieces and germs can easily defeat your purposes. Keep the stapler, tape, paints and glue handy—and *never* underestimate the talents of children. Our projects are designed to motivate your students, encourage environmental awareness and stimulate the creative minds of everyone involved.

Enjoy!

Sincerely,

Jo Jo Cavalline and Jo Anne O'Donnell

Tips and Suggestions

Altoids containers make great keepsake boxes.

Berry baskets make excellent storage containers. To decorate, just weave yarn or thin paper strips through the holes in the sides of the basket.

Butter/margarine tub lids can be used to make stencils for any patterns you want children to trace and cut out. The plastic cuts easily, it's easy for children to hold and it will last longer than paper and won't tear.

Caps and lids can be used for game pieces or markers. Find five alike and use to play tic-tac-toe.

Use 10 caps from pump tooth-paste containers to make bowling pins. Set them up on a desk and use a mar-ble for the ball. Keep score. You can put a square of felt under the pins, too.

Collars and cuffs from old shirts can be used to make bookmarks. The cuffs make nice bracelets, too. Decorate them anyway you want.

Deodorant bottles (roll-on type) can be refilled with white glue and used like a glue stick.

Detergent bottles have endless possibilities. Have you ever considered a race car? Collect extra lids for the wheels.

Dog and cat food cans make just-the-right-size paint containers.

Dried-out magic markers make great paintbrushes!

Egg cartons were meant to be used as sorting trays. The plastic kind make good paint holders, seed starter pots and eyeballs for puppets and masks. The paper kind can eventually be soaked and used for molded paper projects.

Foam peanuts and other shaped packing material make great stuffing for life-sized My Body figures, grocery bag dolls or beanbag furniture for your reading corner. You can also string the white, disc-shaped kind on fishing line for snowflakes.

Tips and Suggestions

Grocery bags make good bodies for dolls. They also make great pinatas; over-the-head masks; vests and a super mummy costume if you have the time, masking tape and a willing victim. (Do not wrap tightly. When complete, carefully cut open the back for easier ins and outs.)

Grocery bags also make ideal folders.

Cut open along one side.

Cut away bottom.

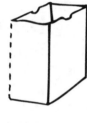

Cut remaining sheet in half.

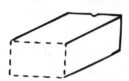

Fold up and over.

Holders can be made out of clothespins. Just glue a picture onto one side and a magnet onto the other.

Ice cream tubs (especially the plastic ones) are terrific storage containers for the classroom. Not bad flowerpots, either.

Junk is in the eye of the beholder.

Kitchen spice racks and jars make great storage areas for art supplies. Jars with shaker tops are great for glitter.

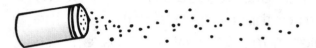

Linoleum tiles are easy to set down and clean up for art projects. Children can have their own tile to work on. If a project needs to be carried from art table to shelf (perhaps it needs to dry overnight), the tile is a firm enough base to serve as a tray. Of course, you can always incise the tiles and make great prints.

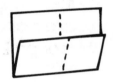

Meat trays (wash thoroughly) can be turned into lacing cards. Just use a hole punch to create designs in the center or space holes evenly around the outside edge. Old shoelaces are great for lacing, or wrap tape around the ends of string or yarn.

New shirts often have a cardboard piece at the collar that will make an outstanding moustache.

Tips and Suggestions

Oven mitts can be used for a great game of indoor catch. Cover the fingers and palm area with adhesive strips of spiney Velcro®. Cover a Ping-Pong™ ball with adhesive strips of fuzzy Velcro®. Save for a rainy day.

Plastic bags (thin strips) can be braided for friendship bracelets.

Q-tips™ have an infinte number of uses.

Reduce. Reuse. Recycle. Repeat.

Shirt cardboard should never be thrown away.

Tissue boxes (the upright kind) can be turned into story-starter containers. Write opening lines or suggestions on adding machine tape. Roll it up and lay in the bottom of the upright box. Pull the story starters through the lid of the box. Keep it on your desk for a "Now what do we do?" opportunity.

Umbrellas make great mobiles. Write poems or haiku on raindrop shapes and hang from the tips of the spines and create a rainy day poetry display.

Velcro® is worth saving. Cut or peel it off whatever you're throwing away.

Wipe-off tissues for dry-erase boards or chalkboards can be made from used

fabric softener dryer sheets.

X rays for dolls can be made from old film negatives. Black-and-white is especially effective.

Yarn scraps can be saved in a ball. Tie ends together and start rolling. It's a convenient way to store the loose pieces and the rainbow effect adds color to your projects requiring yarn.

Zipper-type plastic bags can be washed and reused.

Dear Parent,

We are emphasizing recycling in our curriculum this year. We have a year-long activities program that makes use of recycled materials and we'll be using and discussing the items as we create crafts and other objects.

It would be very helpful if you could save some items for us and bring them to school for our use. The items should be clean (we recommend washing with an antibacterial soap) and free from small parts or sharp edges. The checklist below identifies those items for which we have a particular need at this time.

Your assistance is greatly appreciated.

Thank you!

Your child's teacher

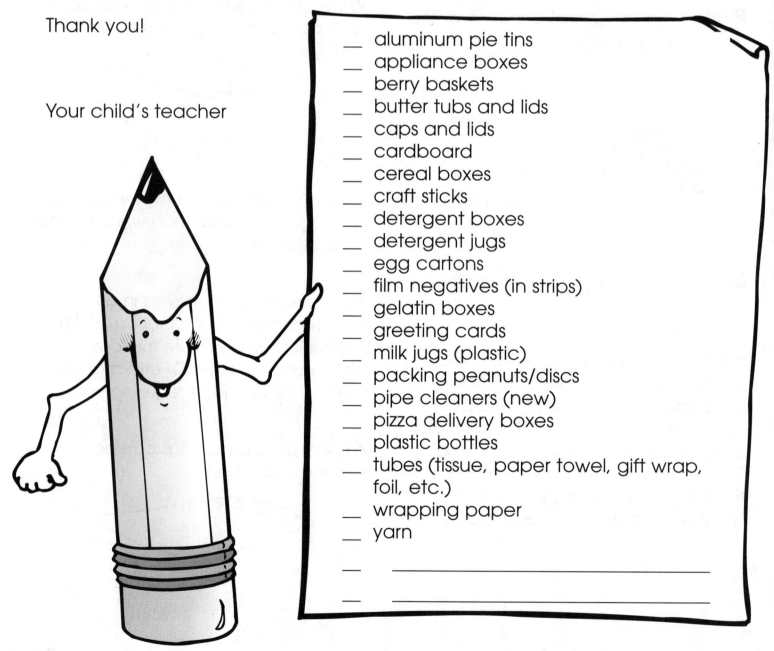

__ aluminum pie tins
__ appliance boxes
__ berry baskets
__ butter tubs and lids
__ caps and lids
__ cardboard
__ cereal boxes
__ craft sticks
__ detergent boxes
__ detergent jugs
__ egg cartons
__ film negatives (in strips)
__ gelatin boxes
__ greeting cards
__ milk jugs (plastic)
__ packing peanuts/discs
__ pipe cleaners (new)
__ pizza delivery boxes
__ plastic bottles
__ tubes (tissue, paper towel, gift wrap, foil, etc.)
__ wrapping paper
__ yarn
__ _____
__ _____

x

Organizers

Materials

plastic milk jug

two plastic pop lids

one film cap

pipe cleaners or thin
  paper strips

scissors

glue

Cut.

Literature Selection

This Farm Is a Mess
by Leslie McGuire
Parents Magazine Press, 1994

Selected Activity

The milk jug holder can be used to
keep pencils, crayons or markers in
order. Lost and found items can be
placed in the milk jug holder, or use it
to hold tokens or rewards.

Directions

1. Cut the milk jug as shown. Glue
   on plastic pop lids for eyes.

2. Glue on film cap for nose.

3. Attach pipe cleaners or thin strips
   of paper for whiskers.

Variations

By changing the way you cut the
ears, this cat can easily become a
dog, rabbit, mouse or reindeer!

1

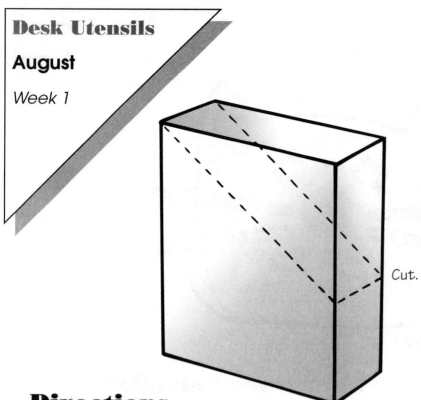

Cut.

Materials
cereal boxes
wrapping paper
labels
scissors
glue
markers

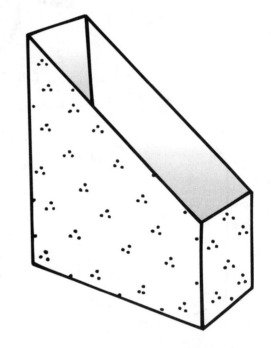

Directions
1. Cut cereal boxes as shown.
2. Cover with wrapping paper.
3. Affix labels.

Variations
1. In addition to recycling wrapping paper, children can make their own wrapping paper by drawing or stamping on grocery bags.
2. Attach boxes to the side of the desks for mailboxes.

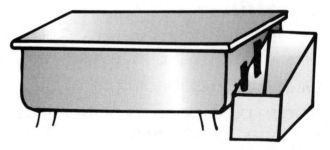

Literature Selection
Fritz and the Mess Fairy
by Rosemary Wells
Dial, 1991

Selected Activity
Use these files to hold drill sheets, students' work or unit materials or to categorize books.

2

Materials

plastic berry baskets
yarn or thin paper strips

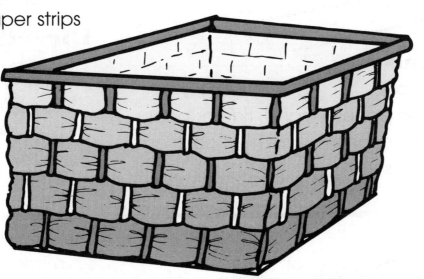

Directions

Weave yarn or colored paper strips in and out of the holes in the berry basket.

Variations

1. Use your school colors. Create stripes of red, white and blue for a patriotic basket. Use red, pink and white for Valentine's Day, etc.
2. Weave up and down instead of around.

Literature Selection

The Berenstain Bears and the Messy Room
by Stan Berenstain
Random House, 1983

Selected Activity

Use the berry basket to store rewards or tokens, as a clay holder, crayon holder or to contain individual art supplies.

Read-Treat: A Day at the Beach

Materials

appliance box
construction paper
markers or crayons
plastic bottles
doll
scissors
glue

box lid (large)
sand, rice or beans
variety of caps and
  lids
detergent box
  (trunk type)
brown paper
rope

Directions

1. Cut away top, bottom and two sides of the appliance box. (Save scraps!)

2. Make ocean waves and a sun from construction paper, or draw them on the box with crayons or markers.

3. Cut out a boat, sail, fish and shells from colorful plastic bottles. Use the patterns on page 7. Attach to the diorama board. Place a doll in the boat.

4. Turn the box lid upside down and fill with sand, rice or beans. Colorful caps can represent seashells. Place your beach in front of the diorama.

Treasure Chest

5. Make a treasure chest by covering a trunk-type detergent box with brown paper. Add handles from rope. Use the chest to house beach-book treasures.

Variation

Add beach chairs and make this beach your reading center for a while.

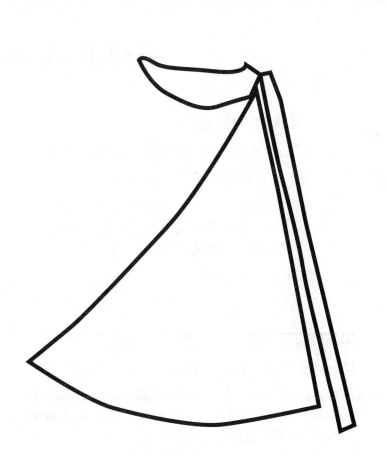

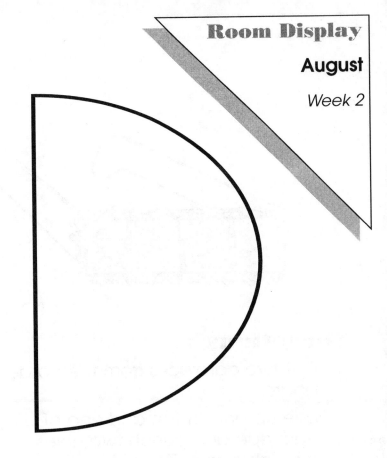

Literature Selections

A Beach for the Birds
by Bruce McMillan
Houghton-Mifflin, 1993

Emma at the Beach
by James Stevenson
Greenwillow, 1990

Max and Diana and the Beach Day
by Harriet Ziefert
Harper & Row, 1987

The Seashore Book
by Charlotte Zolotow
HarperCollins, 1992

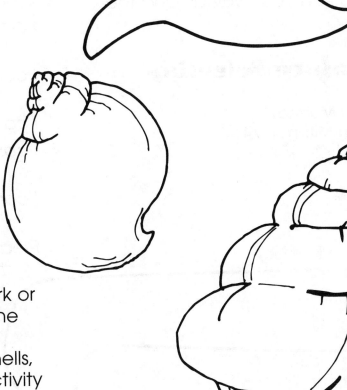

Selected Activity

Children who finish their seat work or other activity early may, "go to the beach." You can embellish the scene with beach towels, real shells, lemonade, etc. See the next activity for some "shades" to wear.

Jokleys

Materials

6" (15 cm) strip of film negatives

yarn (assorted colors)

two 6" x 3" (15 x 8 cm) pieces of thin cardboard (soda box, panty hose card, etc.)

hole punch

Directions

1. Cut two earpieces from the cardboard.
2. Line up end of film and end of earpiece and punch two holes through each. Repeat for the other side.
3. Lace yarn through the holes in the film. Attach the earpieces as you stitch your way around the film.

Literature Selection

Willis
by James Marshall
Houghton-Mifflin, 1974

Selected Activities

Remind students that the minute they put on their Jokleys, a magical sense of creativity comes over them! Begin with this poem:

I put on my glasses and what do I see?

I'll tell you everything, so listen to me.

Incorporate any topic you wish, here are a few suggestions . . .

I can see the forest even through the trees,

I can see the tiniest stripe on a far-away bumblebee.

I can see forever on a cloudy day,

I can see every star in the heavens, I can see the Milky Way!

I can see the Queen of England, sitting down to tea.

Please excuse me, I must go . . . she just invited me!

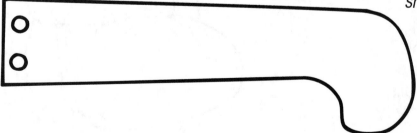

(This information is from various books in our classroom, students are asked to put on their Jokleys and complete the sentence.)

Fill in the missing dinosaur.

I see _____ stretching to eat a tree.

I see _____ looking as mean as can be.

I see _____; he weighs 85 tons.

I see _____ flying up to the sun.

I see _____ stealing a dinosaur egg.

I see _____ stretching his big back legs.

(This activity can be adapted to a variety of subject areas and ability levels.)

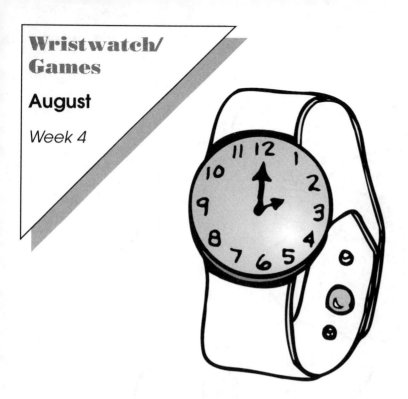

Which Watch?

Materials

plastic milk jug *with cap*

lots of extra caps

indelible white marker

hole punch

brad fastener

craft knife

scissors

tape

Directions

1. Cut around the neck of the milk jug as shown. (*Do this part yourself or get other adults to help. This is too difficult for children. It's easiest to start with a craft knife and then switch to scissors.) Make straps about 3/4" (2 cm) wide and 3 1/2" (9 cm) long.

Cut.

Use a hole punch to make holes 1/2" (1.25 cm) apart at the end of each strap.

2. Write clock-face numerals around the edge of the caps with white marker. Draw hands to show the desired time.

3. Strap the watch onto child's wrist and close with brad fastener. (Top of brad should face the skin, and points should face out. Cover the open points with tape to avoid scratches.)

Literature Selections

Keeping Time
by Franklyn M. Branley
Houghton-Mifflin, 1993

My First Look at Time
"A Dorian Kindersley Book"
Random House, 1991

The School Bus Comes at Eight O'Clock
by David McKee
Hyperion, 1994

Time to . . .
by Bruce McMillan
Lothrop, Lee & Shepard, 1989

10

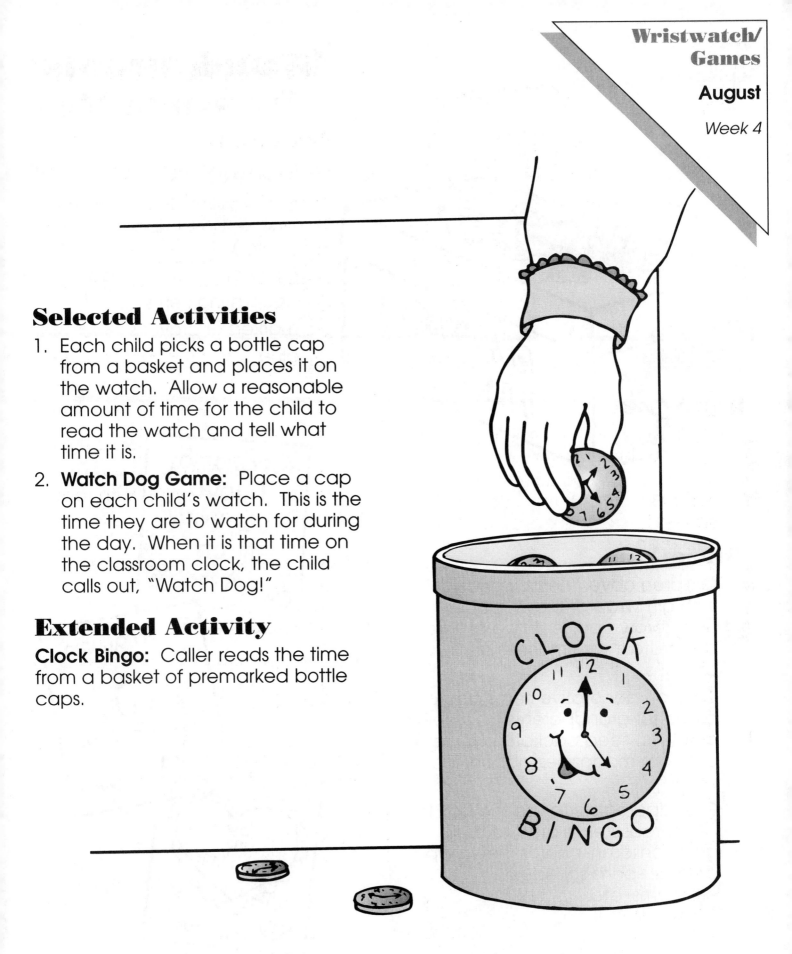

Selected Activities

1. Each child picks a bottle cap from a basket and places it on the watch. Allow a reasonable amount of time for the child to read the watch and tell what time it is.

2. **Watch Dog Game:** Place a cap on each child's watch. This is the time they are to watch for during the day. When it is that time on the classroom clock, the child calls out, "Watch Dog!"

Extended Activity

Clock Bingo: Caller reads the time from a basket of premarked bottle caps.

Grandparents' Treasure Box

Materials

box with lid (detergent box, shoe box, cupcake box, etc.)

gift wrap or brown paper

decorating items

markers or crayons

glue

Directions

1. Children cover the box and lid with gift wrap or brown paper. If using brown paper, have children decorate it with markers or crayons.

2. Glue on decorative items appropriate for grandparents (seashells, golf tees, seed packets, pictures cut from magazines, ribbon, lace, etc.).

3. Grandparents can use the box to keep treasures related to their grandchildren–photos, newspaper articles, sports schedules, programs, etc.

12

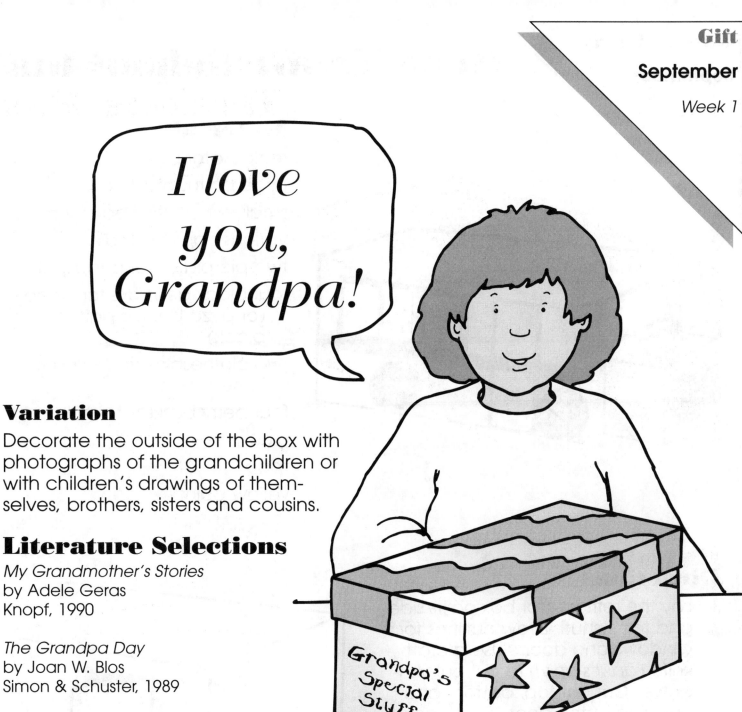

I love you, Grandpa!

Variation

Decorate the outside of the box with photographs of the grandchildren or with children's drawings of themselves, brothers, sisters and cousins.

Literature Selections

My Grandmother's Stories
by Adele Geras
Knopf, 1990

The Grandpa Day
by Joan W. Blos
Simon & Schuster, 1989

Selected Activity

Have children write a poem to paste on the outside of the treasure box or on the inside of the lid.

Read Treat: School Bus

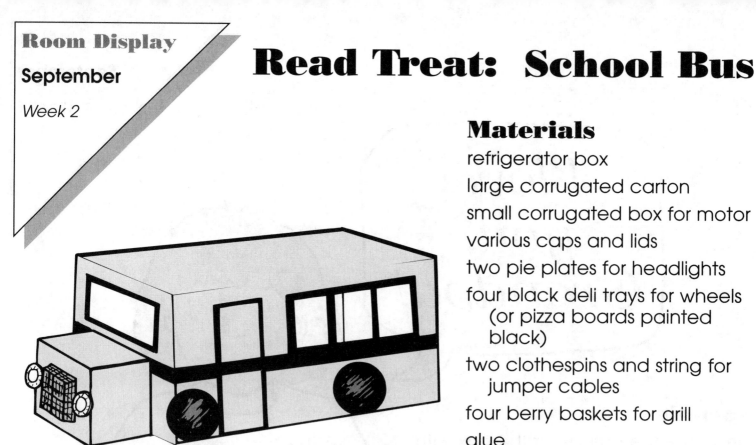

Materials

refrigerator box

large corrugated carton

small corrugated box for motor

various caps and lids

two pie plates for headlights

four black deli trays for wheels
(or pizza boards painted
black)

two clothespins and string for
jumper cables

four berry baskets for grill

glue

tape

yellow paint

Directions

1. Lay the refrigerator box on its side
and tape shut. Draw outlines for
windows and door.   Use a craft
knife (*adults only!*) to cut out windows. Cut out top, bottom and
one side of the door. Fold back
to open and close.

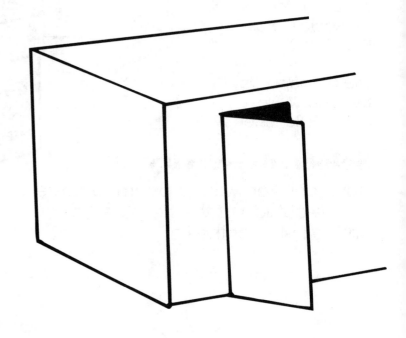

2. Tape the larger corru-
   gated carton to the
   front of the body of
   the bus. Use a craft
   knife to open three
   sides around the top
   for the hood. Attach
   pie plates to either
   side of the front of this
   box for headlights.
   Attach four berry
   baskets to the center
   front for the grill.

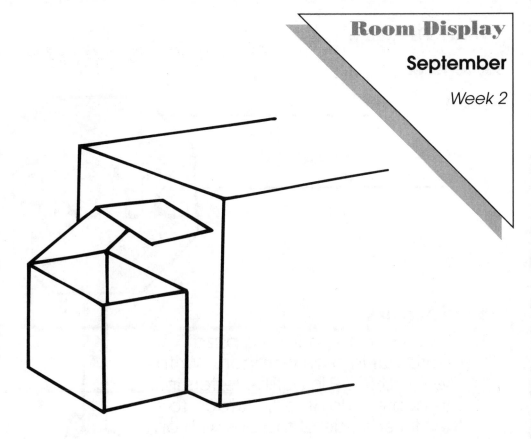

3. Make a motor from a smaller
   corrugated box. Cut off the top.
   Glue on various caps and lids for
   motor and battery parts. Place
   the motor under the hood.

4. Glue on deli trays to the body of
   the bus for wheels.

5. Attach string to clothespins to
   make jumper cables.

6. Paint school bus yellow. Add
   black stripes along the sides;
   paint black frames around the
   windows.

Variations

1. Make a stop sign from a pizza board cut into an octagon. Write the word *STOP* in outline letters in the center. Paint red. Attach to the driver's side of the bus with an L-shaped strip of corrugated cardboard.

2. You can use this basic shape to create an ice cream truck, ambulance, garbage truck, moving van, etc.

BUS PASS

For _____

Date _____

Selected Activities

Role-play any of the *Magic School Bus* plots. Where would your students like this bus to take them? Create your own *Magic School Bus* story.

This school bus or any other vehicle you create can be used to initiate a lesson on street and traffic safety.

Note

Children will enjoy climbing in the school bus and letting it take them on many reading adventures. You can use the bus pass above to show how many books the student has read. Tokens could be earned during other class activities to be used for a "ride" on the bus.

Literature Selections

The Magic School Bus Series
by Joanna Cole
Scholastic

School Bus
by Donald Crews
Greenwillow, 1984

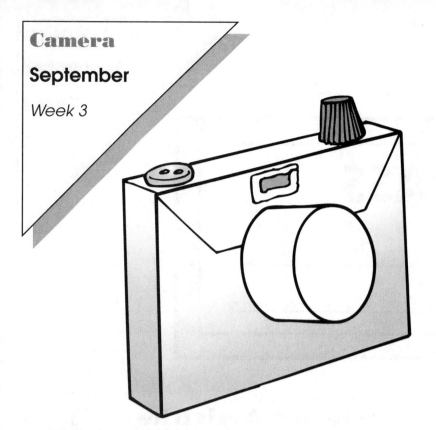

Say Cheese!

Materials

plastic audiocassette case
spray can or detergent jug lid
toothpaste cap
button
pipe cleaner
glue

Directions

1. Hold the cassette case so that the "spine" is at the top and the hinged back faces front. The cassette case will be the body of the camera.

2. Glue the spray can lid or the detergent jug lid to the front of the cassette case. This is the lens.

3. With the lid/lens facing out and the back of the camera to the viewer, glue a small button on the top right of the case. Glue the toothpaste cap on the top left of the case.

4. A small piece of pipe cleaner can serve as the viewfinder.

Variation

Glue an end of string to either side of the case for a carrying strap.

Literature Selections

Grandpa Baxter & the Photographers
by Caroline Castle
Orchard, 1993

Simple Pictures Are the Best
by Nancy Willard
Harcourt, 1978

Selected Activities

A real camera can add a lot to your lessons. For example:

1. Photograph items with the beginning sounds you are studying. Make your own flash cards.

2. Photograph situations for story problems. Write the questions on the back: There are 5 children in the picture, 2 of them . . . .

3. Illustrate your own classroom library books with photographs. Try a well-known story such as "The Three Little Pigs."

4. Take photographs during the school day. Allow students to take the photos home and share with their families some of the great things going on in your classroom. Suggest to parents that they send photos to share what great things are going on at home!

5. Don't forget the value of photographs in your students' assessment portfolios.

6. Invite a professional photographer to visit your class.

Student Portfolios

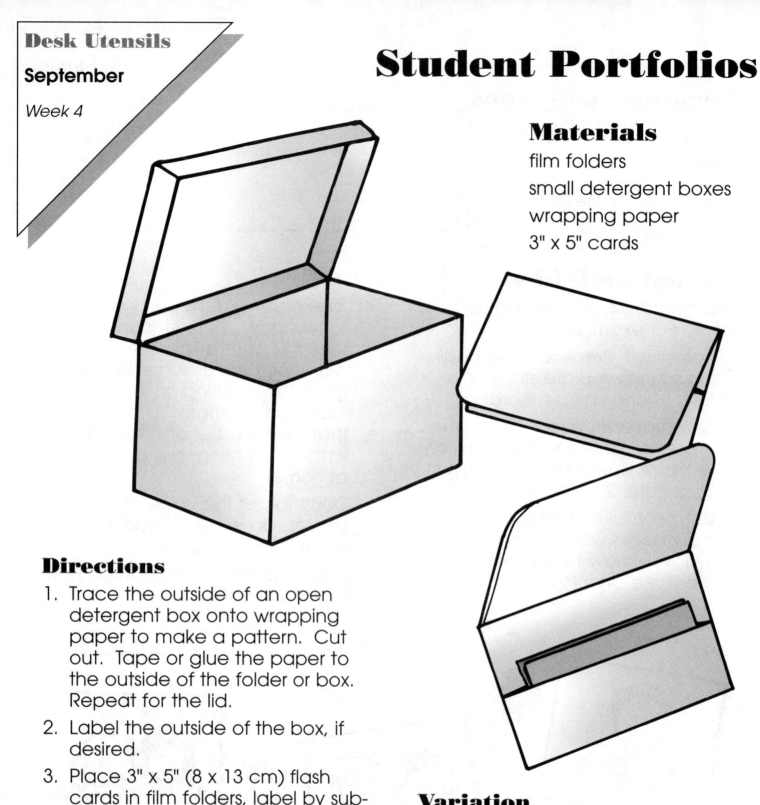

Materials
film folders
small detergent boxes
wrapping paper
3" x 5" cards

Directions

1. Trace the outside of an open detergent box onto wrapping paper to make a pattern. Cut out. Tape or glue the paper to the outside of the folder or box. Repeat for the lid.

2. Label the outside of the box, if desired.

3. Place 3" x 5" (8 x 13 cm) flash cards in film folders, label by subject area or content (ie. addition facts, spelling words, vocabulary, etc.). Students can turn to their individual portfolios when work is completed early or other times during the day.

Variation

If you don't want to cover the box with wrapping paper, you can have the students cover the boxes with masking tape or colored tape and then decorate with stickers or markers.

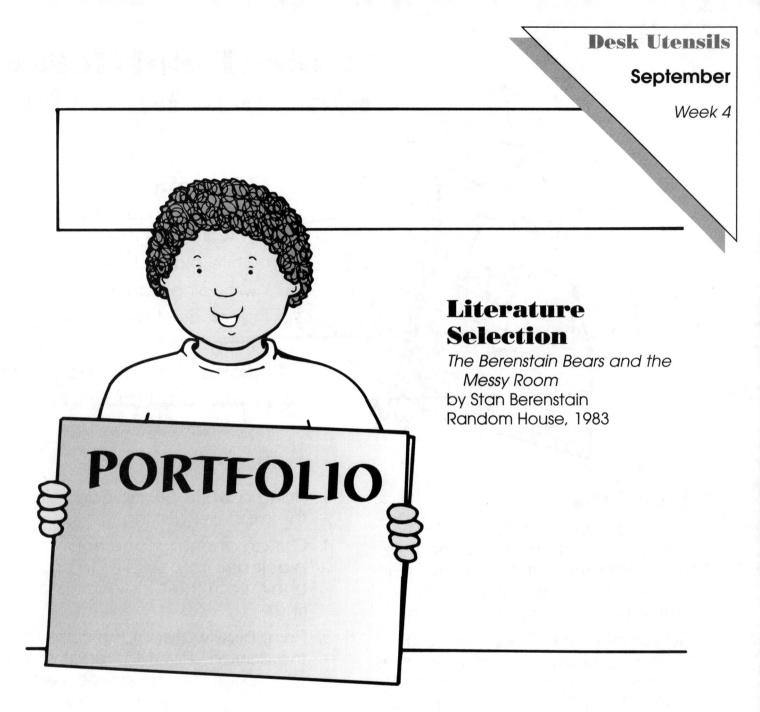

Literature Selection

The Berenstain Bears and the Messy Room
by Stan Berenstain
Random House, 1983

Selected Activities

Use for: picture portfolios
math facts
spelling words
vocabulary words
daily assignments
award certificates
assignments

Note

See "Tips and Suggestions"
(pages vii-ix) for other organizers.

Read-Treat: Columbus Day Ship

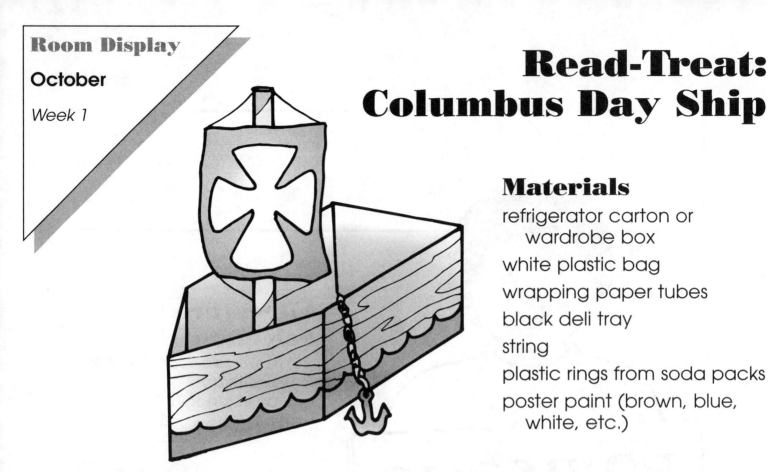

Materials

refrigerator carton or wardrobe box

white plastic bag

wrapping paper tubes

black deli tray

string

plastic rings from soda packs

poster paint (brown, blue, white, etc.)

Directions

1. Lay the carton on its side. Leave the back end open. Cut off the top. Fold the cut-off piece in half to make the prow of the boat. Tape to the front of the carton.

2. Make a mast by taping several cardboard wrapping paper tubes end to end. Make 2" to 3" (5 to 8 cm) slits at 1" (1.25 cm) intervals around one end. Spread open and tape the mast to the bottom of the boat, at about the center.

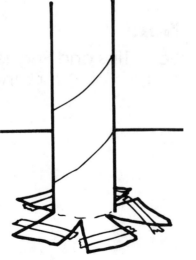

3. Hang a white plastic bag sail from the mast using string.

4. Cut an anchor shape from a black deli tray. Make an anchor chain from the plastic soda pack rings.

5. Paint blue water at the base of the carton. Paint the boat brown with black lines for a wood effect.

Variations

1. Students can design their own ships using shoe boxes, detergent boxes, etc.

2. Research the ships Columbus sailed on his first voyage. Try to incorporate as many of your findings as possible in the construction of your ship.

Literature Selections

Christopher Columbus
by Ann McGovern
Scholastic, 1989

In Fourteen Ninety-Two
by Jean Marzollo
Scholastic, 1991

A Picture Book of Christopher Columbus
by David A. Adler
Holiday House, 1991

Selected Activity

Assign students various duties on board the ship. Have them keep a daily journal.

Extended Activity

Learn as many nautical terms and phrases as appropriate for your students. Label the parts of the ship.

United Nations Day

Materials

large pizza box
blue poster paint
white cardboard
large white paper plate
glue
wrapping paper tube
aluminum foil
tape

Directions

1. Open the pizza box and lay it flat. Trim to make a large rectangle.

2. Paint one side of the box with the blue poster paint. Let dry.

3. Cut out olive branches from the white cardboard using the patterns on page 25.

4. Copy the continents pattern on page 26 and paste onto the white paper plate.

5. Center the paper plate on the blue rectangle and glue in place. Glue olive branches onto the rectangle on either side of the plate.

6. Cover the wrapping paper tube with aluminum foil.

7. Attach the wrapping paper tube to the left side of the flag and display on your bulletin board.

Variations

1. Paint and decorate both sides of the pizza box. Tape several wrapping paper tubes together to make a taller flagpole. Display in your school hallway.

2. Collaborate with other classrooms, and make a flag for each of the member nations of the United Nations.

Literature Selection

Search for Peace: The Story of the U.N.
by William Jay Jacobs
Atheneum, 1994

Selected Activity

Create a country and design a flag to represent it.

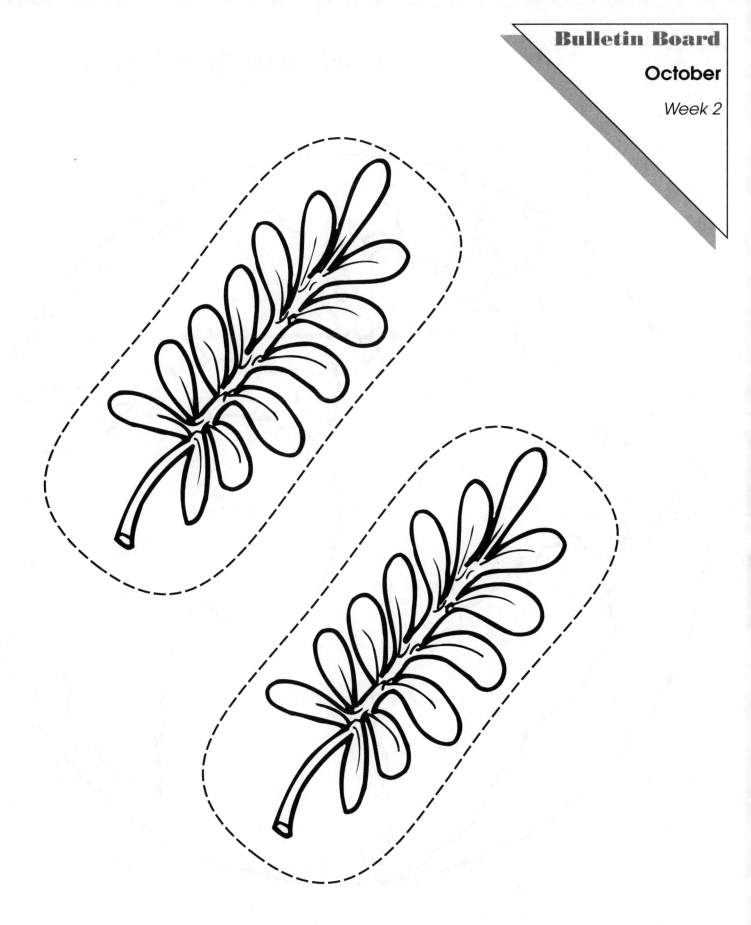

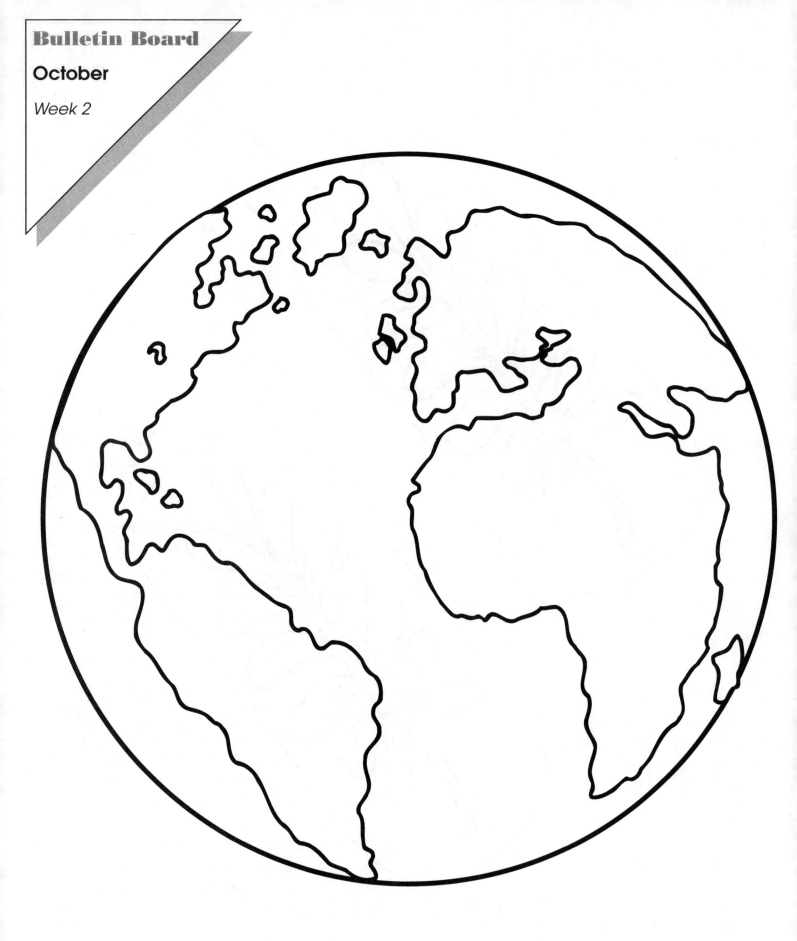

Broomstick

Materials
newspaper
orange plastic bags
paper towel roll
black or orange spray paint
tape

Directions

1. You will need one paper towel roll, one double sheet of newspaper and one orange plastic bag for each broomstick.

2. Spray the paper towel roll with black or orange paint and let dry.

3. Lay the newspaper down flat, fold once and position the fold at the top. Place the orange plastic bag on top of the sheet of newspaper.

4. Cut slits through both the bag and the newspaper. Do not cut all the way up to the fold. Stop about 2" (5 cm) from the top.

5. Starting at one end, tightly roll the newspaper and plastic bag. Secure the roll at the top (folded edge) with tape.

6. Place the taped end of the newspaper into one open end of the paper towel tube. Tape in place.

7. Carefully pull apart the strips of newsprint and plastic bag to complete your broom. (The newsprint will tear easily and younger children may need assistance with this step.)

8. Copy the pumpkin pattern and poem on page 28. Tape to the broomstick.

Swish, swish!
What is that?
A bat? A cat?
A big black hat?

Swish, swish!
Is it a trick?
No, it's a treat . . .
It's my broomstick!

Variation

Create your own patterns and
poems to tape to the broomstick.

Literature Selections

Halloween
by Gail Gibbons
Holiday, 1984

Hey-How for Halloween
by Lee Bennet Hopkins
Harcourt, 1974

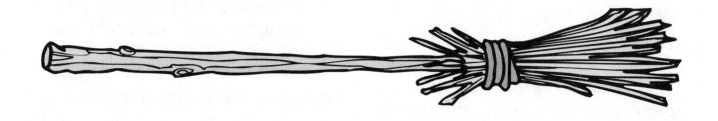

Telescope

Materials

35mm film container with lid

self-adhesive reinforcer rings

dark green or black plastic bag

self-adhesive star stickers

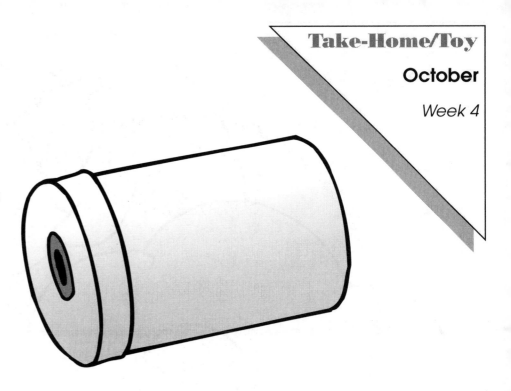

Directions

1. Punch a hole in the center of the lid and the center of the bottom of the film container.
2. Adhere reinforcer rings to film container around each hole.
3. Tape the plastic bag to the student's desk. (If you don't mind the children laying on the floor, it's fun to tape the bags to the underside of the desk.)
4. Place the star stickers on the bag in the patterns of various constellations.

Variations

1. Tape enough bags together to cover a large portion of your ceiling. Create a fairly accurate representation of the night sky.
2. Use glow-in-the-dark star stickers.

Literature Selections

Glow-in-the-Dark Constellations
by C.E. Thompson
Putnam, 1989

Stars, Planets and Galaxies
by Sune Engelbrektson
Bantam, 1975

Telescopes (gr. 5-8)
by Lionel Bender
Watts, 1991

Selected Activities

Follow a constellation as it travels through the night sky. Observe the various positions throughout the year.

Visit a planetarium. Perhaps your community has an astronomy club or expert. Ask them to visit your classroom and share some of their knowledge and experiences.

Children may enjoy taking these materials home and sharing them with family and friends.

Note

Natural History Magazine (published by the American Museum of Natural History, Central Park West at 79th Street, New York, NY 10024) has a monthly column, "Celestial Events," which features timely information on stars and planets and other items of interest.

Election Day

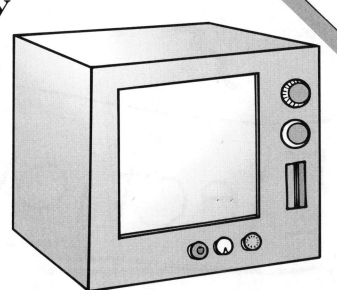

Materials

medium to large card-
board box

aluminum foil or black, gray
or green cellophane
sheet

variety of caps and lids

glue

poster paint

Directions

1. Cut a hole in one side of the box for the screen. (An adult will have to do this for younger children.)

2. Glue on various caps and lids for dials and channel and volume selectors.

3. Paint the box and let dry.

4. Cover the opening with aluminum foil or cellophane.

Literature Selections

Arthur's TV Trouble
by Marc T. Brown
Little, 1995

How Does a TV Work?
by Isaac Asimov
Gareth Stevens, 1992

Voting and Elections
by Dennis B. Fradin
Children's, 1985

Variations

Using the patterns provided, make campaign badges for children.

Selected Activities

Classroom helpers, cafeteria helpers, messengers, board cleaners and paper monitors can be elected positions rather than selected.

Discuss the qualifications of each position and hold nominations. Have the candidates write and deliver a speech, prepare advertisements, posters, etc. Check your local newspapers and TV stations for campaign ideas.

Hold an election. These positions (or others that you may choose) are really active so the winners must carry through with their campaign promises.

If appropriate for your class and grade level, you may wish to continue coverage after these officials have been elected and periodically review their performance.

Read-Treat: Tepee

Materials

heavy string or rope (six
pieces, each long enough
to reach from ceiling
attachment to the floor)

duct tape

large eye hook

lots of brown paper grocery
bags

glue

markers

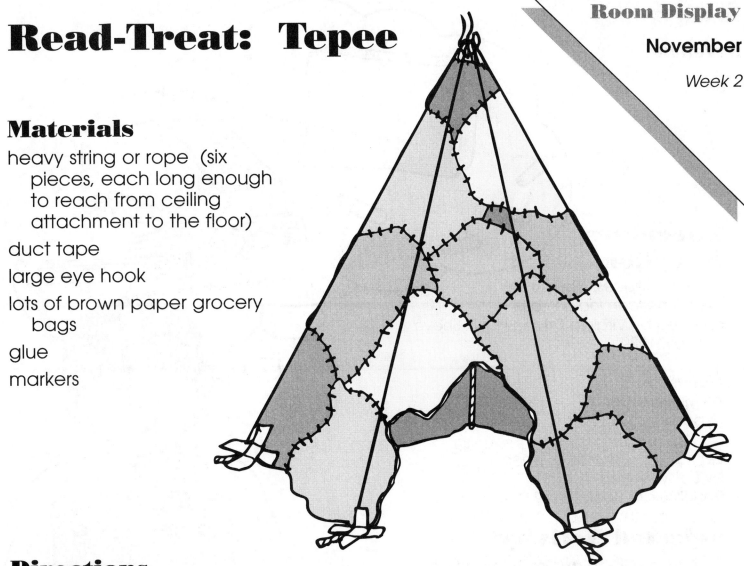

Directions

1. If possible, tie strings to a sturdy grid in a drop ceiling or screw an eye hook into the ceiling in the corner of the room and tie the strings to the hook. If neither of these alternatives is appropriate, use duct tape to secure the strings to the ceiling.

2. Spread out the strings to form the tepee supports and tape to the floor with duct tape. Your tepee should be fairly round. It would be a good idea to identify where the entrance will be at this point.

3. Tear the grocery bags into the shapes of various animal hides. Decorate with markers.

4. Drape the "hides" over the supports and glue together. Continue until tepee is covered. (Don't forget to leave a space for the entrance!) You may wish to add "stitches" with markers.

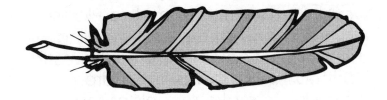

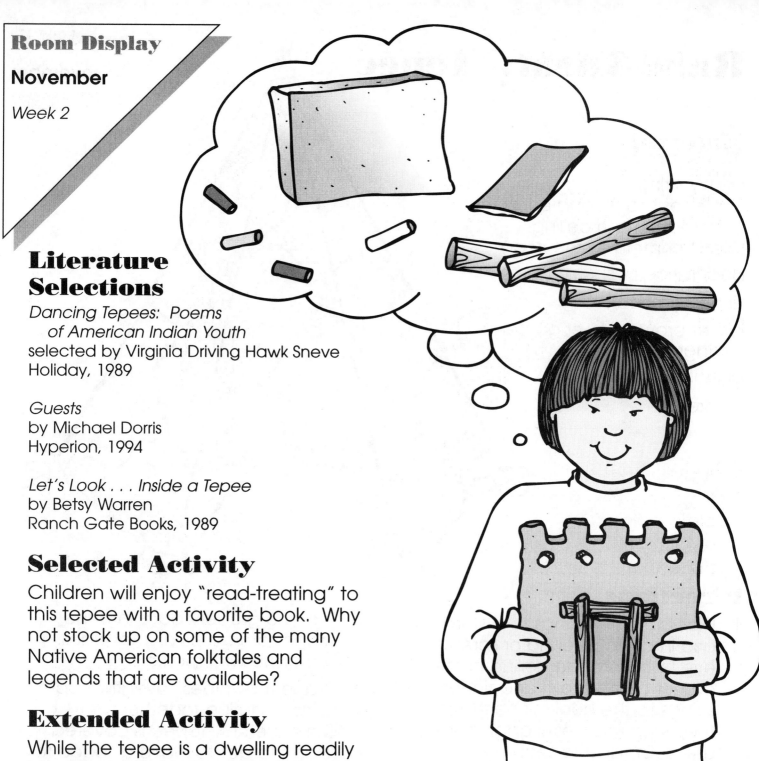

Literature Selections

Dancing Tepees: Poems of American Indian Youth
selected by Virginia Driving Hawk Sneve
Holiday, 1989

Guests
by Michael Dorris
Hyperion, 1994

Let's Look . . . Inside a Tepee
by Betsy Warren
Ranch Gate Books, 1989

Selected Activity

Children will enjoy "read-treating" to this tepee with a favorite book. Why not stock up on some of the many Native American folktales and legends that are available?

Extended Activity

While the tepee is a dwelling readily identified with Native Americans, it may be interesting for your students to look into other types of housing utilized by various tribes. The tepee was well suited to the mobile Plains Indians, but what types of dwelling suited the peoples of the Southwest? Northeast? Northwest? Children may wish to make models of some of these other types of structures.

Rain Stick

Materials

masking tape

paper towel or wrap-
 ping paper tube

paper bag

beans, rice or small
 buttons

string

feathers

beads

Directions

1. Tape one end of the tube com-
 pletely closed.

2. Pour filler (beans, rice or small
 buttons) into the tube. Do not
 fill more than halfway.

3. Tape the open end closed.

4. Cut two circles from the paper
 bag with a diameter 2" to 3" (5
 to 8 cm) larger than the tube.

5. Fit circles onto the ends of the
 tube and tie in place with
 string.

6. Attach feathers and beads to
 the ends of the string.

7. Decorate the tube with paint or
 markers. See page 36 for some
 designs to use.

Variation

1. A more authentic sound
 can be created by first
 pushing nails into the
 tube at random inter-
 vals. Use nails that are
 shorter than the diame-
 ter of the tube so that
 they do not poke
 through. Use about six
 to eight nails for a 12"
 (30 cm) tube. Cover
 the tube with masking
 tape to keep the nails in
 place. *This is not appropriate for younger chil-
 dren.*

2. Substitute old leather
 shoelaces for the string.

35

Literature Selections

Earthmaker's Lodge: Native American Folklore, Activities and Food
edited by E. Barrie Kavasch
Cobblestone Publishing, 1994

The Rainstick: A Fable
by Sandra Robinson
Falcon Press, 1994

Selected Activities

The rain stick has a wonderfully therapeutic and relaxing sound; use it to signal quiet times.

The rain stick is great for sound effects for choral reading.

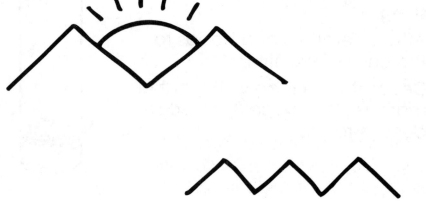

36

Holiday Countdown Calendar

Materials

36" square of butcher paper, construction paper or oaktag

marker

Styrofoam™ meat trays

8 green plastic soda bottles

62 butter tub lids–clear, not opaque

glue

glitter glue

hole punch dots or sequins

yarn

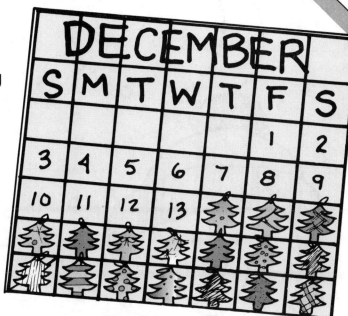

Directions

1. Cut off the top and bottom of a green plastic soda bottle. Cut open lengthwise. Using the pattern on page 39, cut out the tree shape. You can get about four trees per bottle. Make a tree for each child in your class. You will need 31 trees for the calendar.

2. Have children decorate their trees with hole punch dots, glitter glue and/or sequins. Alert young children to sharp edges and supervise carefully.

3. Place the tree inside one of the butter tub lids and add a few loose sequins or dots. Put glue around the outside rim of the lid. Add a small loop of yarn at the top. Cover with the second lid and let the glue dry.

4. Section off the paper or oaktag sheet into 5" (13 cm) squares.

5. Cut 4" (10 cm) letters for DECEMBER and SMTWTFS from Styrofoam™ meat trays. Glue *December* on the top row and the days of the week in the boxes in the second row.

6. Make a December calendar out of the rest of the boxes and tape one of the children's trees in each box.

7. Count down to holidays and other special days in December by removing one tree each day. The child can take the tree home once it's removed.

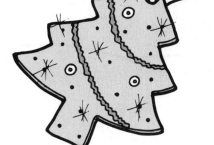

Variations

If you do not wish to use the tree pattern, you can cut out snowflakes, snowpeople, gift boxes or other appropriate shapes.

Literature Selections

A Busy Year
by Leo Lionni
Knopf, 1992

Gather Up, Gather In:
A Book of Seasons
by M.C. Helldorfer
Viking, 1994

When This Box Is Full
by Patricia Lillie
Greenwillow, 1993

Selected Activity

Change the pattern and you can use this calendar idea for any month of the year. Try turkeys in November, hearts in February, shamrocks in March, etc.

Read-Treat: Gift of Reading

Materials

large appliance box

tape

white plastic bags

red and green poster paint

butter tubs or other small, shallow containers

small kitchen or bath sponges

Directions

1. Cut an entrance in each side of the box.
2. Tape the box closed.
3. Paint the box with red poster paint.
4. Cut the sponges into tree shapes.
5. Place a small amount of green paint in the bottom of the butter tub(s).
6. Have children sponge-print green tree patterns all over the outside of the box.
7. Cut the plastic bag into strips and use it to make ribbon and a large bow for your package.

Variations

Use different colors of paint and cut the sponge into other shapes for an endless variety of uses. For example: snowflakes for winter, tulips or umbrellas for spring, suns or sailboats for summer, leaves for fall, cake and candles for a birthday, etc.

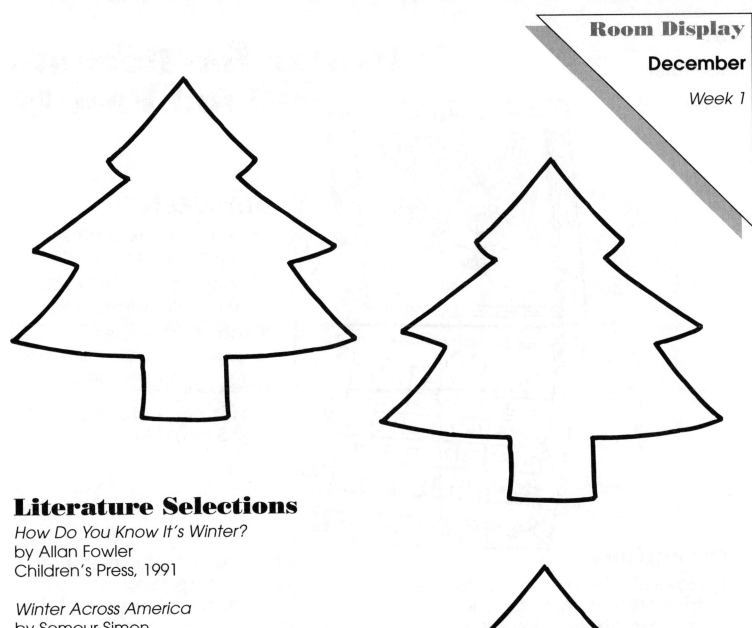

Literature Selections

How Do You Know It's Winter?
by Allan Fowler
Children's Press, 1991

Winter Across America
by Semour Simon
Hyperion, 1994

Winter Poems
selected by Barbara Rogansky
Scholastic, Inc., 1994

Selected Activity

Children can spend a cozy time in this winter "read-treat." Just supply them with plenty of good wintry books and maybe a pillow or two and a quilt.

Calendar for Parents and Family

Materials

large pizza box or other recycled cardboard

12 sheets of 8½" x 11" (22 x 28 cm) drawing paper

12 calendar pages

staple

hole punch

plastic bag cut into long 1" (2.5 cm) strips

Directions

1. Have children draw one picture for each month on the sheets of drawing paper. Make sure the pictures are horizontal. Tape onto the inside of the pizza box lid.

2. As an alternative to making your own calendar pages, see if your local bank or some other institution will donate enough calendars for your class. Then tape the calendar pages to the inside of the pizza box bottom.

3. Punch holes in the perimeter of the pizza box, spacing about 1" (2.5 cm) apart. Lace strips of plastic bag through the holes to make a decorative edge.

42

I like it when it snows.
It tickles my cheeks
and my nose.
It sparkles in the
bright sunlight.
And looks like diamonds
in the night.

Literature Selections

Chicken Soup with Rice
by Maurice Sendak
Harper & Row, 1962

Farm Boy's Year
by David McPhail
Atheneum, 1992

Thirteen Moons on a Turtle's Back
by Joseph Bruchac and Jonathan Landon
Philomel, 1992

Selected Activity

Children can fill in special dates on their calendar pages–birthdays, family celebrations, recitals, school events, vacations, etc.

Extended Activity

Older children may wish to write a poem for each month and illustrate it.

Kwanzaa Mat

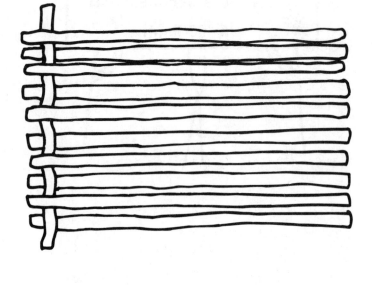

Materials

plastic bags cut into 1" (2.5 cm) wide strips (traditional Kwanzaa colors are red, green and black), some strips should be about 14" (36 cm) long and others about 19" (48 cm)

Directions

1. Most standard-size place mats are about 12" (30 cm) high and 17" (43 cm) long. It'll probably be easiest to weave the mat by putting the lengthwise strips in position and then weaving the shorter pieces up and down.

   Place about 15 of the long strips in front of you, horizontally. Alternate colors.

2. Weave the shorter strips up and down, again alternating colors.

3. Tuck in the ends by folding over and pushing under the next piece.

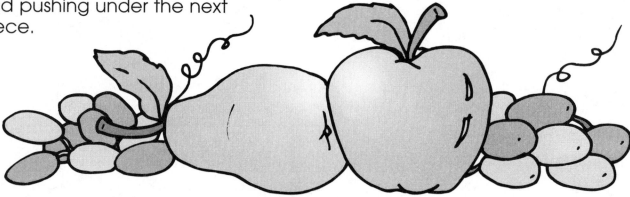

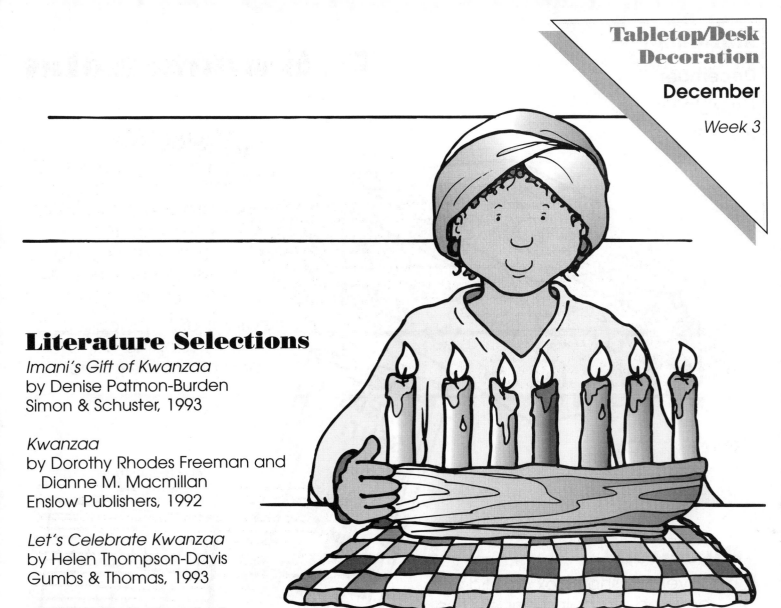

Literature Selections

Imani's Gift of Kwanzaa
by Denise Patmon-Burden
Simon & Schuster, 1993

Kwanzaa
by Dorothy Rhodes Freeman and
    Dianne M. Macmillan
Enslow Publishers, 1992

Let's Celebrate Kwanzaa
by Helen Thompson-Davis
Gumbs & Thomas, 1993

Selected Activity

A Kwanzaa mat is placed on a table under the seven candles which represent the seven principles celebrated during the seven days of the holiday. These seven principles are called Nguzo Saba (ngoo-zoo sah-bah). Have your class find out what the seven principles are.

Thank-You Notes

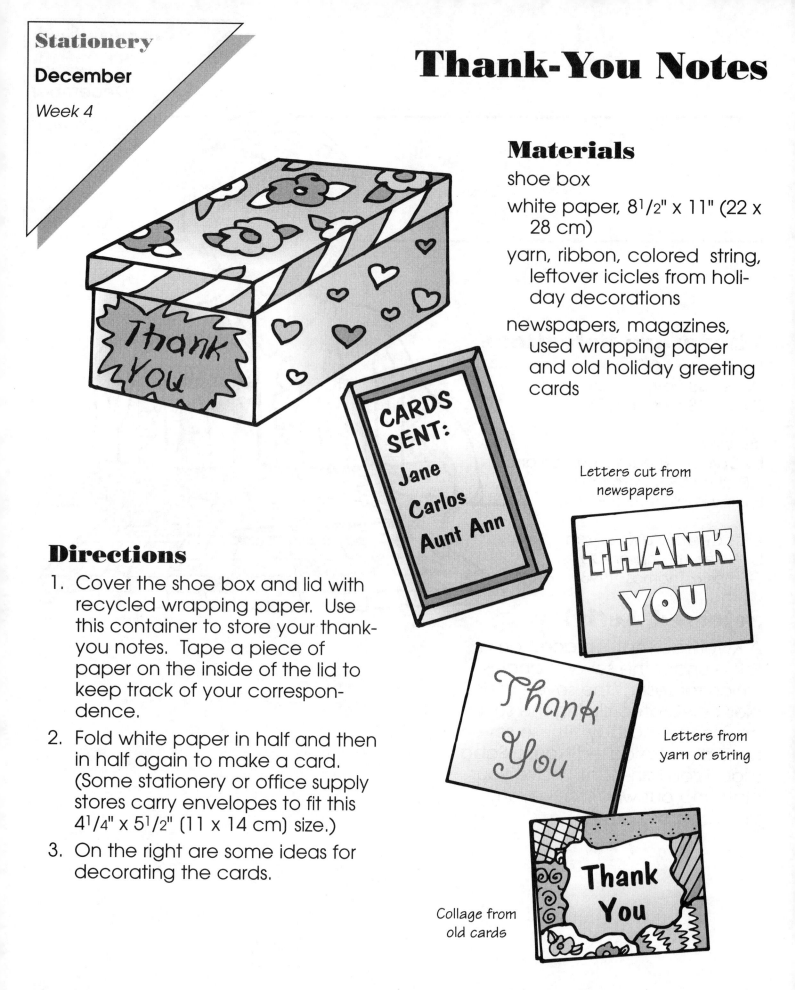

Materials

shoe box

white paper, 8 1/2" x 11" (22 x 28 cm)

yarn, ribbon, colored string, leftover icicles from holiday decorations

newspapers, magazines, used wrapping paper and old holiday greeting cards

CARDS SENT:
Jane
Carlos
Aunt Ann

Letters cut from newspapers

THANK YOU

Thank You

Letters from yarn or string

Collage from old cards

Thank You

Directions

1. Cover the shoe box and lid with recycled wrapping paper. Use this container to store your thank-you notes. Tape a piece of paper on the inside of the lid to keep track of your correspondence.

2. Fold white paper in half and then in half again to make a card. (Some stationery or office supply stores carry envelopes to fit this 4 1/4" x 5 1/2" (11 x 14 cm) size.)

3. On the right are some ideas for decorating the cards.

Thank you, Aunt Jean!

Literature Selection

Thank You, Amelia Bedelia
by Peggy Parrish
HarperCollins, 1993

Selected Activity

At this time of year, children are probably most concerned with responding to those relatives and friends with whom they have exchanged holiday gifts. You might also want to discuss sending thank-yous to: parents who have helped out, classroom visitors, custodians, substitute teachers, aides and volunteers, principal, bus drivers, crossing guards, etc.

Dr. Martin Luther King, Jr. Day

Materials

two-liter plastic soda bottle
cardboard

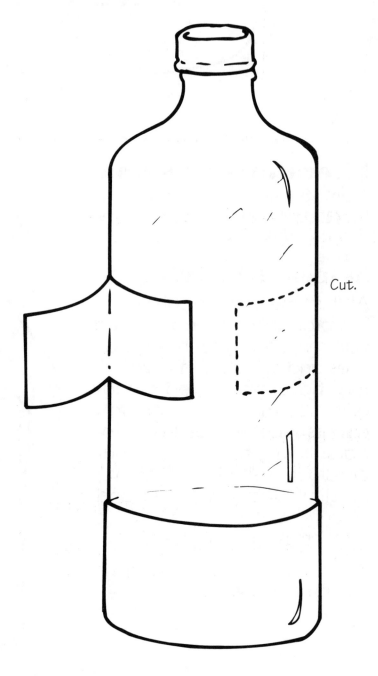

Cut.

Directions

1. Cut parallel slits into the plastic bottle with a craft knife (*adults only!*). Slits should be about 1" (2.5 cm) apart and run from the side of the bottle to just about the center. See illustration.

2. Photocopy the book, shirt and Martin Luther King patterns on page 49. Glue to cardboard and cut out. Fold the book.

3. Tape or glue the face to the shirt. Then glue this piece to the lid of the bottle. Glue the book to the "arms."

48

Literature Selection

Families: Poems Celebrating the African American Experience
selected by Dorothy S. and Michael R. Strickland
Boyds Mill Press, 1994

Happy Birthday, Martin Luther King
by Jean Marzollo
Scholastic, Inc., 1993

Selected Activity

Discuss Martin Luther King's famous, "I have a dream" speech. On slips of paper, have children write simple statements representing dreams that they have. Place the slips of paper in the soda bottle at the opening created by the arms.

49

Roman Jewels

Materials

- string, yarn or plastic bags cut into strips
- Styrofoam™ meat trays
- Styrofoam™ packing peanuts or discs
- toothpaste caps
- pop tabs
- plastic bottles in various colors
- milk cap rings
- glitter
- glue

Directions

1. Cut various gem shapes from Styrofoam™ meat trays. Here are a few suggestions.

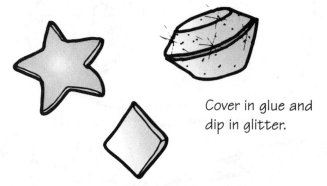

Cover in glue and dip in glitter.

2. Other jewels can be created as follows:

toothpaste caps   pop tab   packing disc dipped in glitter

3. String jewels onto yarn, string or thin strips of plastic bags.

4. Here are some things you can make:

Braid plastic bag strips into a "friend-ship" bracelet. Add jewels as you go along.

milk cap ring with "jewel"

Literature Selection

A Cache of Jewels
by Ruth Heller
Grosset & Dunlap, 1987

Selected Activity

Janus was the Roman god of beginnings, endings, openings and closings. Janus was pictured as having two faces, one looking forward and one looking back. The Janus festival was held on January 1. Julius Caesar decreed that this festival would mark the beginning of the year. The festival was a huge celebration in Rome and noisemakers of all sorts were used to celebrate. Romans wore lots of jewelry and marched in the streets. Your students may wish to celebrate the new year with a parade. Load up on the jewelry and perhaps even parade into another classroom!

Extended Activity

Make Janus festival posters. At the top draw a picture of two faces, one looking forward and one looking back. Have your students come up with things they remember from the past year to list under the backwards-looking face. List the things they are looking forward to or hope for under the forward-looking face.

Read-Treat: Build an "Egg"loo

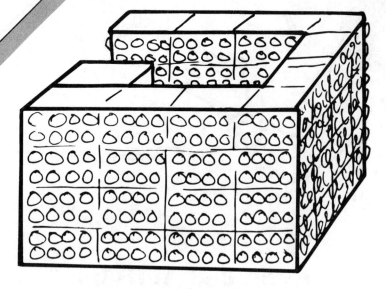

Materials

half-gallon milk cartons

white egg cartons

white paper or white spray paint

glue

Directions

1. Flatten the spout end of the milk carton and tape closed.

2. Wrap the entire milk carton in white paper or spray paint it white.

3. Trim the egg carton so you have a piece that fits one side of the milk carton. Eight cups (two rows of four) should work.

4. Glue the egg carton to two opposite sides of the milk carton. Keep two sides of the carton flat for better stacking.

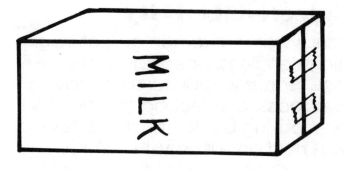

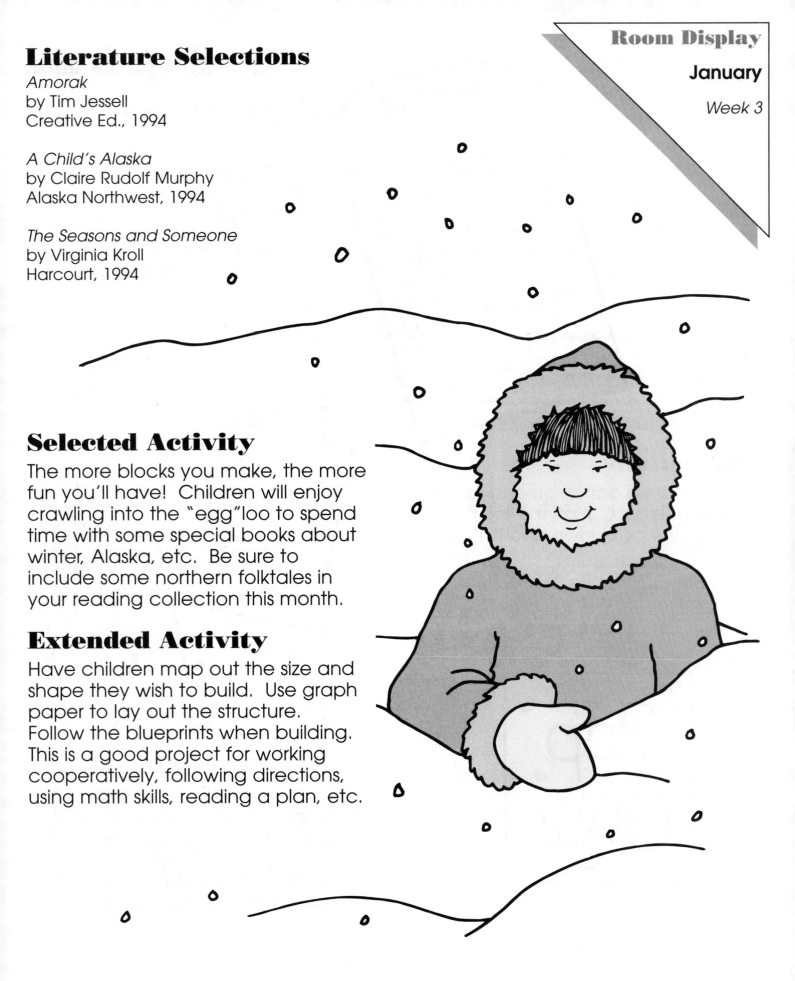

Literature Selections

Amorak
by Tim Jessell
Creative Ed., 1994

A Child's Alaska
by Claire Rudolf Murphy
Alaska Northwest, 1994

The Seasons and Someone
by Virginia Kroll
Harcourt, 1994

Selected Activity

The more blocks you make, the more fun you'll have! Children will enjoy crawling into the "egg"loo to spend time with some special books about winter, Alaska, etc. Be sure to include some northern folktales in your reading collection this month.

Extended Activity

Have children map out the size and shape they wish to build. Use graph paper to lay out the structure. Follow the blueprints when building. This is a good project for working cooperatively, following directions, using math skills, reading a plan, etc.

Pop Quiz

Materials

cardboard soda can cartons

cardboard sheets from 24-pack soda cartons

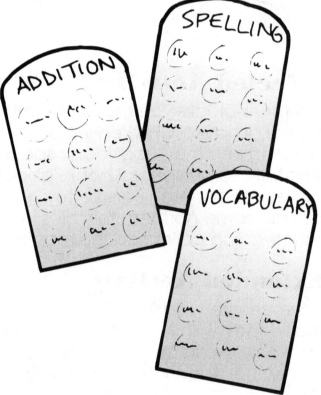

Directions

1. Stand the carton on end so that it is vertical. Cut off the top and cut the box down about 1" (2.5 cm).

2. Round off the tops of the cardboard sheets. Use the areas created by the depressions in the cardboard to write in all kinds of quiz questions.

3. Children can write their responses directly onto the card, or you can use answer sheets. Set up self-checking charts.

Literature Selection

The First Grade Takes a Test
by Miriam Cohen
Harper, 1983

Selected Activity

You might want to offer the children an opportunity to earn a can of soda for completing 10 cards.

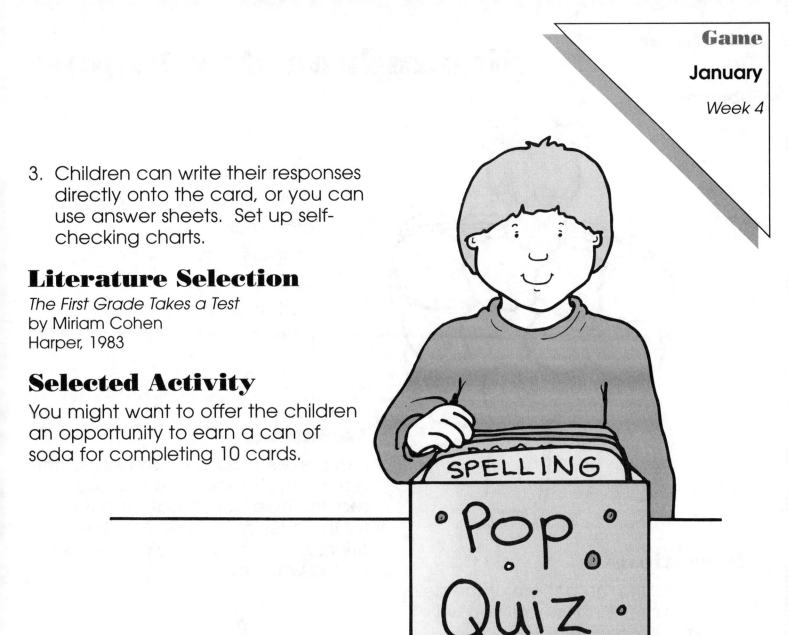

Groundhog Day Puppet

Materials

half-pint round deli container
craft stick
markers or crayons
scissors
cotton balls
glue

Variations

Make eyes, nose and whiskers for the groundhog's face. You can use sequins, hole punch dots or buttons for the eyes and nose. Add thread, string, broom straw or pipe cleaners for the whiskers.

Directions

1. Cut a slit in the bottom of the deli container. This is where you will insert the craft stick.

2. Copy the groundhog face pattern on page 57. Color and cut out.

3. Glue the face to the end of the craft stick. Set aside to let dry.

4. Cover the outside of the deli container with glue and attach cotton balls.

5. Insert the end of the craft stick into the slit and pull through until the groundhog's head reaches the bottom of the cup and is hidden. Will he see his shadow? Push up on the stick . . . did he?

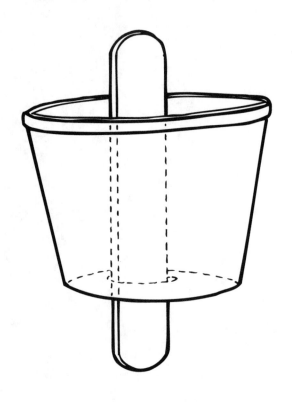

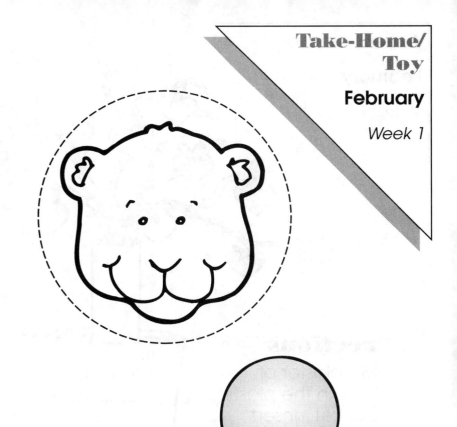

Literature Selections

*Do Not Disturb: The Mysteries of Animal
  Hibernation and Sleep*
by Margery Facklam
Little, 1989

How Do You Know It's Spring?
by Allan Fowler
Children's Press, 1991

Selected Activity

Use a flashlight to make shadows on
the wall. Create a short shadow
play using finger shadows or stick
puppets.

Extended Activity

Play shadow tag outdoors. Choose
one player to be IT. IT tries to step on
other players' shadows to get them
out.

Read-Treat: Poet-Tree

Materials

heavy cardboard tube from a roll of carpeting

plastic bucket

plaster of Paris

real tree branches (not too dry)

margarine or butter tub lids

Styrofoam™ meat trays

Directions

1. Mix plaster of Paris in the plastic bucket. Insert one end of the carpet tube and let harden.

2. Make heart-shaped stencils from the butter tub lids.

3. Use the stencils to trace lots and lots of Styrofoam™ heart shapes onto the meat trays. Use a variety of colors or color with markers. Cut out the heart shapes.

4. Tape real tree branches to the top of the carpet roll.

5. Children read a short poem to the class. Tape it to one of the heart shapes and hang it on a branch of the tree.

Variations

1. Children can sign their names to the tree trunk after they've read the poem.

2. Children can go to the tree during story time (or at other times), and read one of their classmate's poems.

Literature Selections

Time to Rhyme: A Rhyming Dictionary
by Marvin Terban
Boyds Mill Press, 1994

A Tree in the Wood
by Christopher Manson
North-South Books, 1993

Selected Activity

Children can choose to read a poem they have found or they may wish to write an original poem. This activity lends itself quite well to couplets, limericks, haiku and other short poetic forms.

Extended Activity

The tree trunk has many possibilities for year-round activities. Cover the trunk with paper. Add some new branches and you're ready for the next season!

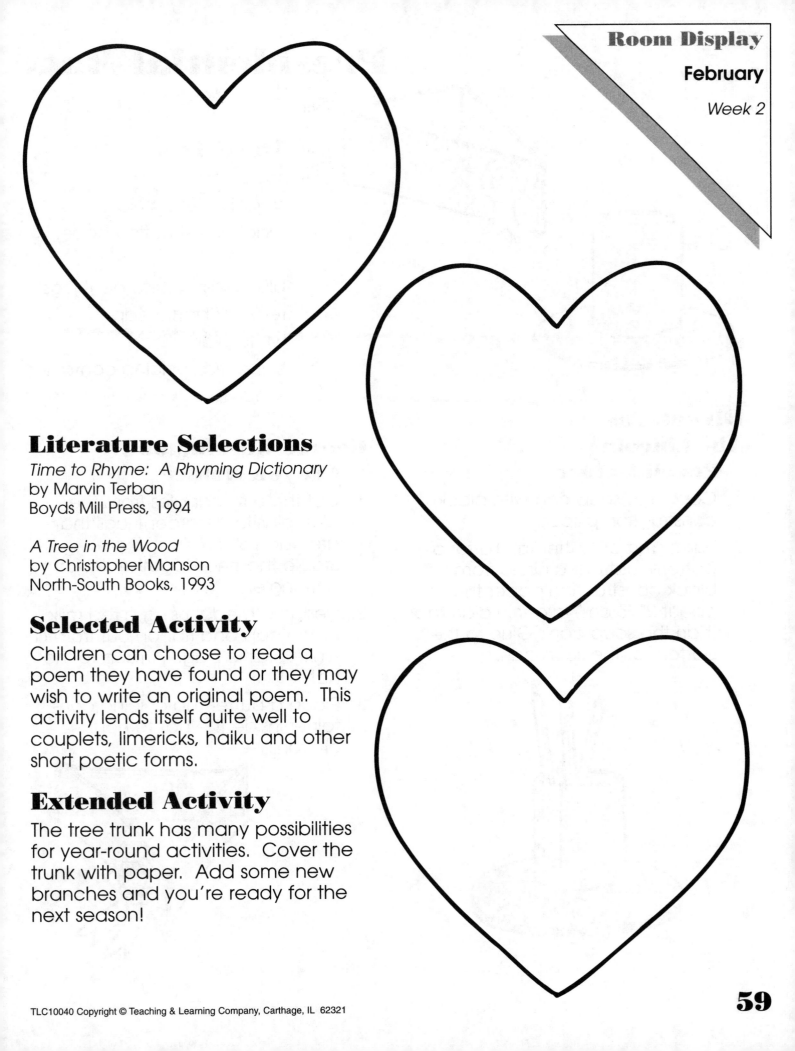

Presidential Hats

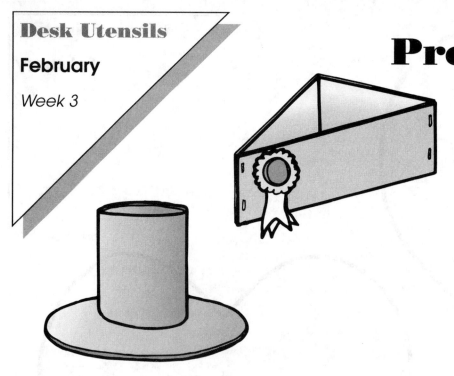

Materials

soup can
small butter tub lid
black construction paper

blue plastic detergent jugs
red milk bottle cap
white plastic bag
butter tub or icing container

Directions
Abe Lincoln
Pencil Holder

1. Cover the soup can with black construction paper.

2. Using a small butter tub lid for a pattern, cut out a circle from black construction paper that is about 2" (5 cm) larger in diameter than the soup can. Glue to the bottom of the soup can.

George Washington
Crayon Holder

1. Cut three rectangles from the blue plastic detergent jugs that are each 3" x 6" (8 x 15 cm). Staple the ends together to form a triangle.

2. Design a medal using a red milk bottle cap and ribbon cut from a white plastic bag. Attach to the hat.

3. Place a butter tub or icing container inside the hat to hold crayons.

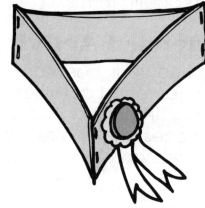

Literature Selections

George Washington: A Picture Book
by James C. Giblin
Scholastic, 1992

George Washington's Cows
by David Small
Farrar, Strauss & Giroux, 1994

A Picture Book of Abraham Lincoln
by David A. Adler
Holiday House, 1989

Selected Activity

You can adapt the directions for the desk utensils to create hats your students can wear. Make Abe Lincoln's stovepipe hat and George Washington's three-cornered hat out of construction paper. Let your students celebrate Presidents' Day with a presidential parade.

A Betsy Ross Flag

Materials
white plastic
detergent bottles
red plastic lids
white plastic lids

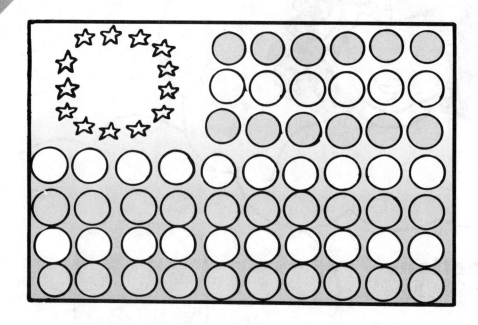

Directions
1. Cut 13 white stars from white plastic detergent bottles. Use the pattern on the right.

2. You can glue the plastic lids onto a piece of butcher paper and hang on your wall or bulletin board, or you can use pushpins to create the flag directly onto your bulletin board. Alternate rows of red and white caps to make the stripes.

Literature Selection
Betsy Ross
by Alexandra Wallner
Holiday House, 1994

Selected Activity
Students can put up a lid or row of lids as a reward or when finished with seat work early.

Star
Cut 13.

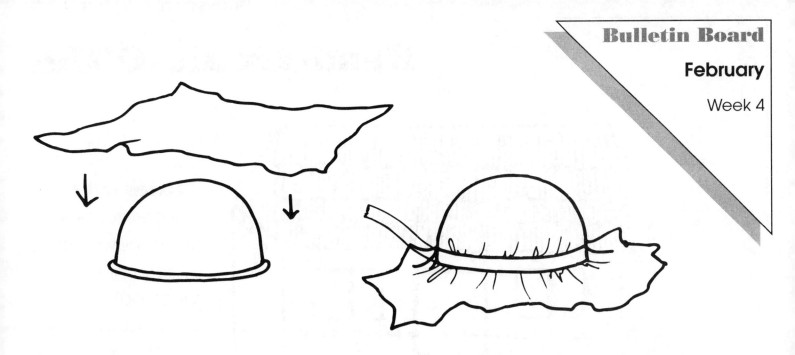

Extended Activity

Make these clever Betsy Ross hats for your students to wear. For each hat you'll need:

- plastic grocery bag
- masking tape
- mixing bowl

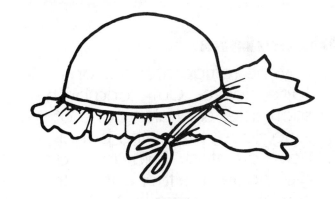

Place the plastic grocery bag over the inverted mixing bowl. Tape around the outside of the bag just above the rim. Scrunch the plastic as you go around to form gathers. Trim the bag about 1¹/₂" (4 cm) from the tape. Remove from bowl.

Read-Treat: O'Hut

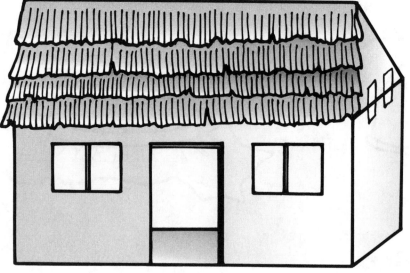

Materials
refrigerator box
lots of newspapers
tape or glue
white paint

Directions

1. Lay the refrigerator box on its side. Tape closed. Cut along both short sides and along one of the long sides. Lift up the panel you have created. Fold down a triangle shape at either end of the panel (see illustration). Tape the base of the triangle to the side of the box to hold in place. This is the roof of your o'hut.

2. Cut out front and back doors for the hut and several windows.

3. Paint the hut white.

4. Place double sheets of newspaper so that the fold is at the top. Cut into strips about 1" (2.5 cm) wide. Do not cut all the way to the fold; stop about 2" (5 cm) from it.

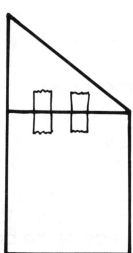

5. The newspaper fringes will make the hut's thatched roof. Tape the newspaper to the cardboard in rows. Start at the bottom of the roof and work your way up to the top.

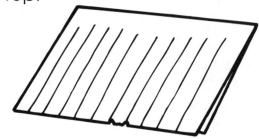

Literature Selection

How a House Is Built
by Gail Gibbons
Holiday, 1990

Selected Activity

Imaginations will run wild as you discuss Ireland and its many legends of leprechauns, rainbows and pots of gold. The O'Hut makes an inviting place for students to read some of these stories alone or in small groups.

Snake!

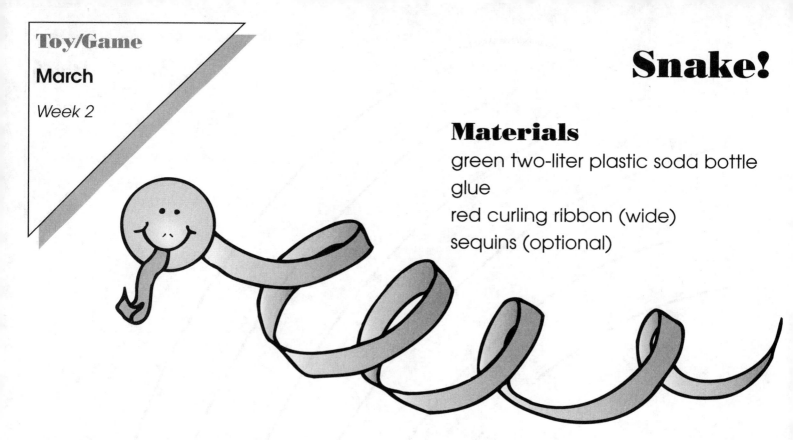

Materials

green two-liter plastic soda bottle

glue

red curling ribbon (wide)

sequins (optional)

Directions

1. Cut off the hard plastic bottom of the bottle.

2. Start at the bottom and cut a continuous strip about 1" (2.5 cm) wide. Stop as you reach the neck of the bottle.

3. Photocopy the snake face on page 67 and glue to the cap (or draw your own snake face directly onto the cap).

4. Glue a 3" to 4" (8 to 10 cm) piece of ribbon to the snake's tongue and curl or use the tongue pattern on page 67.

Variation

Give your snake sequin eyes.

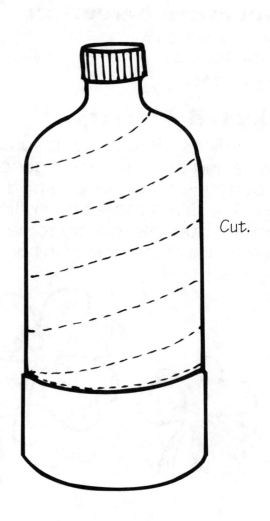

Cut.

Tongue

Literature Selection

Snakes
by Seymour Simon
HarperCollins, 1993

Selected Activities

The legend says that St. Patrick chased all the snakes from Ireland–which must be how they found their way into your classroom! Try hiding the snakes in and around the room. Have one child or a team of children find them and chase them out of "Ireland."

Play a game of tag. If you're caught, you're out of Ireland! The winner can wear a leprechaun crown. To make it you'll need:

shamrocks cut from green Styrofoam™ meat trays and 2" (5 cm) band of paper to fit around the child's head

Tape shamrocks to the paper band.

Children could also earn shamrocks for individual crowns by completing assignments, great behavior, helping out with classroom chores, etc.

Money Tree

Materials

large plastic flowerpot
clay or plaster of Paris
real tree branch
plastic or paper money

Directions

1. Trim small branches off the bottom of your tree branch so that you have a "trunk" of about 6" to 8" (15 to 20 cm).

2. If your flowerpot has a hole in the bottom, close it off securely. Mix plaster of Paris in the flowerpot.

3. Position the tree trunk in the center of the plaster-filled flowerpot, and hold for a few moments while the plaster begins to harden.

4. Glue plastic or paper money to the branches of the tree.

5. Make 10 to 15 different trees. This is a good activity for small groups. Give each group a different amount of money to glue on their tree.

Variation

Open paper clips to form hangers. Glue the money to hangers and hang on the tree branches.

Literature Selections

The Story of Money
by Betsy Maestro
Mulberry Books, 1995

26 Letters and 99 Cents
by Tana Hoban
Greenwillow, 1987

Selected Activity

Children can count the money on the different trees and determine which has the most, the least, more bills than coins, more coins than bills, the same amount but different configurations, etc.

Use hangers rather than gluing the money directly onto the tree for children who have difficulty keeping track of what they have counted. This way, they can pick the money off the tree as they count.

April Fool's Fun

Materials

small plastic containers with snap-on lids (powdered drink mix, film container, frosting can, etc.)

strips of construction paper, any color, about 1" (2.5 cm) wide

paper to cover container

glue

markers

4. Cover the container with paper, and glue in place. Use a marker to make a label for the outside of the container: CANDY, MONEY, SURPRISE, etc.

5. Deliver to an unsuspecting recipient. When the lid is opened, out jumps the paper spring!

Directions

1. Fold a paper spring out of the construction paper strips. Make sure the paper spring is at least two times the height of the container.

2. Copy one of the "surprise" faces from page 71. Glue it to one end of the paper spring.

3. Place the paper spring in the container, with the surprise face on top. Gently push it down and snap on the lid.

Glue ends to form a V. Alternate folding strips over each other.

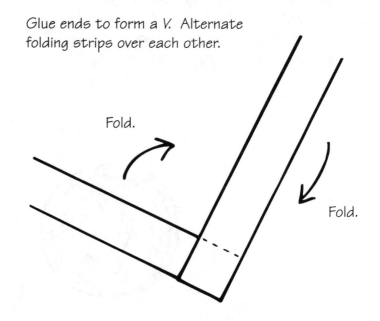

Fold.

Fold.

Literature Selection

April Fool's Day
by Emily Kelley
Carolrhoda Books, 1983

Selected Activity

Students may wish to make more than one surprise container. Ask them to keep track of the reactions as they give out their April Fool's gifts. Students can use this material for a short story, a reaction graph, a poem or picture, etc.

Read-Treat: Gone Fishing

Materials

large cardboard box

paints

rocks

2' to 3' (.6 to .9 m) feet of blue felt

dowel rod

ribbon spool

string

plastic lid (or plastic scraps from soda bottles, etc.)

magnet

paper clips

Styrofoam™ meat trays or cardboard

Directions

1. Cut a large cardboard box as shown.

2. Paint your favorite fishing spot on the cardboard background.

Cut.

3. Cut the blue felt into an irregular shape for the fishing hole.

4. Edge the fishing hole with rocks.

5. Make a fishing pole by attaching the ribbon spool to one end of the dowel rod. Tie the string onto the other end.

6. Cut a fishing hook from the plastic lid or plastic bottle scrap. Glue a magnet onto the hook. Attach hook to the end of the string.

7. Cut fish shapes from meat trays or cardboard. Color and attach a paper clip to each. Place in the pond.

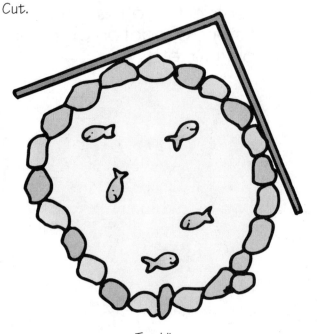

Top View

72

Literature Selections

Fish Is Fish
by Leo Lionni
Pinwheel Books, 1970

Life in a Pond
by Camelita Robinson
Golden Press, 1967

Over in the Meadow
by Ezra Jack Keats
Scholastic, 1975

Selected Activities

Make as many fish as you wish and use them for a variety of curriculum activities. Write math problems on the fish. When children catch the fish they have to solve the problem in order to keep the fish. Write vocabulary words on the fish. A correct definition or using the word in a sentence keeps the fish. Etc.

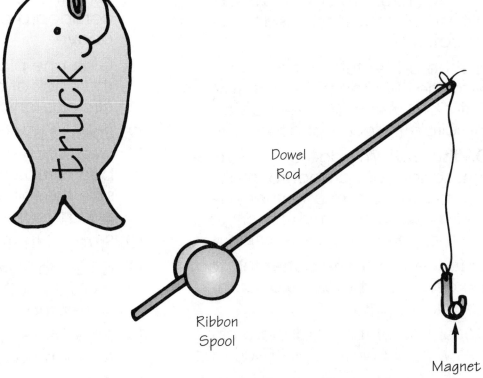

Motorcycle

Materials

two long wrapping paper tubes (about 20" (51 cm) in length)

cardboard (pizza box)

butter tub

Styrofoam™ meat tray

aluminum foil

ribbon (1" (2.5 cm) wide x about 30" (76 cm) long)

colored paper

yellow paint or marker

silver spray paint

Directions

1. Use the butter tub to trace four circles onto the cardboard. Also draw a 9" (23 cm) square and four ½" x 4" (1.25 x 10 cm) strips. Cut out these pieces. Set aside. See illustration A.

2. Use the butter tub to trace a circle onto the Styrofoam™ meat tray. Cut it out and paint one side of the circle yellow. Set aside.

3. On the bottom edge of the 9" (23 cm) square of cardboard, measure in 2½" (6 cm) on either side and mark. Cut from the mark to the top corner. See illustration B.

4. Glue the top of the butter tub to the center of the piece of cardboard. Set aside.

5. Cover two of the cardboard circles with aluminum foil. Glue one of the cardboard strips to each of the four circles. Set aside.

6. Measure about 4" (10 cm) down from the top of the wrapping paper tube and bend firmly. Do the same with the second tube.

7. Glue the tubes to either side of the cardboard piece. See illustration above.

8. Glue one plain cardboard circle to the back of one foil-covered circle, aligning the paper strips.

9. Spread the strips so that one fits over each side of the bent cardboard tube handlebars. Make sure the foil circle faces the driver, and glue the strips in place.

10. Spray with silver paint.

11. Glue the Styrofoam™ circle (yellow side out) to the bottom of the butter tub.

12. Attach thin strips of colored paper to each handlebar.

13. Attach ribbon to either side of the back of the cardboard piece; adjust length on each child.

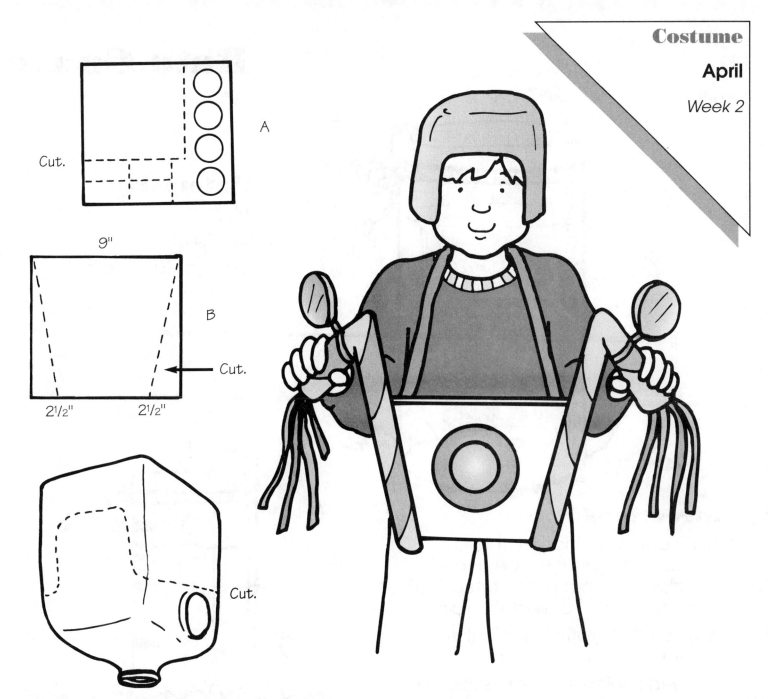

A

Cut.

9"

B

Cut.

2½"   2½"

Cut.

Literature Selections

The Mouse and the Motorcycle
by Beverly Cleary
Dell, 1965

Runaway Ralph!
by Beverly Cleary
Dell, 1981

Note: These stories are also available on video from ABC Kidtime Videos.

Selected Activities

Give directional words to students as they ride their motorcycles: left, right, north, south, U-turn, stop, yield, etc. Set up a course and make traffic signs.

Take a motorcycle trip and turn your excursion into story problems calculating distance, time, etc.

Make a helmet from the bottom of a gallon milk jug. Discuss safety rules, signs, precautions.

Rain Gauge

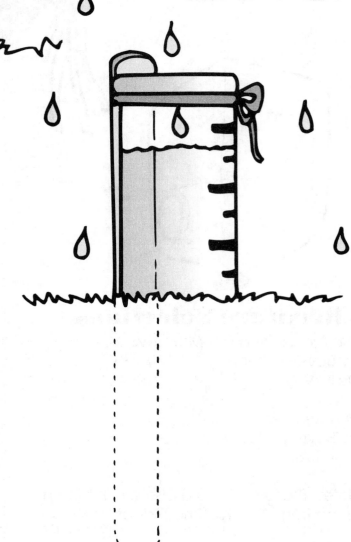

Materials

ruler
craft stick
spice jar (clear glass)
string

Directions

1. Select a location for the rain gauge where it will be undisturbed but not so sheltered that it's unable to collect the rain.
2. Insert the craft stick into the ground about halfway.
3. Tie the spice jar to the stick with string.
4. Place the ruler in the spice jar to measure the rainfall.

Variations

1. Use an indelible marker to draw measurements on the side of the jar.
2. Attach jar to the outside of your classroom window (make sure it is not under an overhang).

Literature Selections

Bringing the Rain to Kapiti Plain
by Verna Aardema
Dial, 1981

A Rainy Day
by Sandra Markle
Orchard Books, 1993

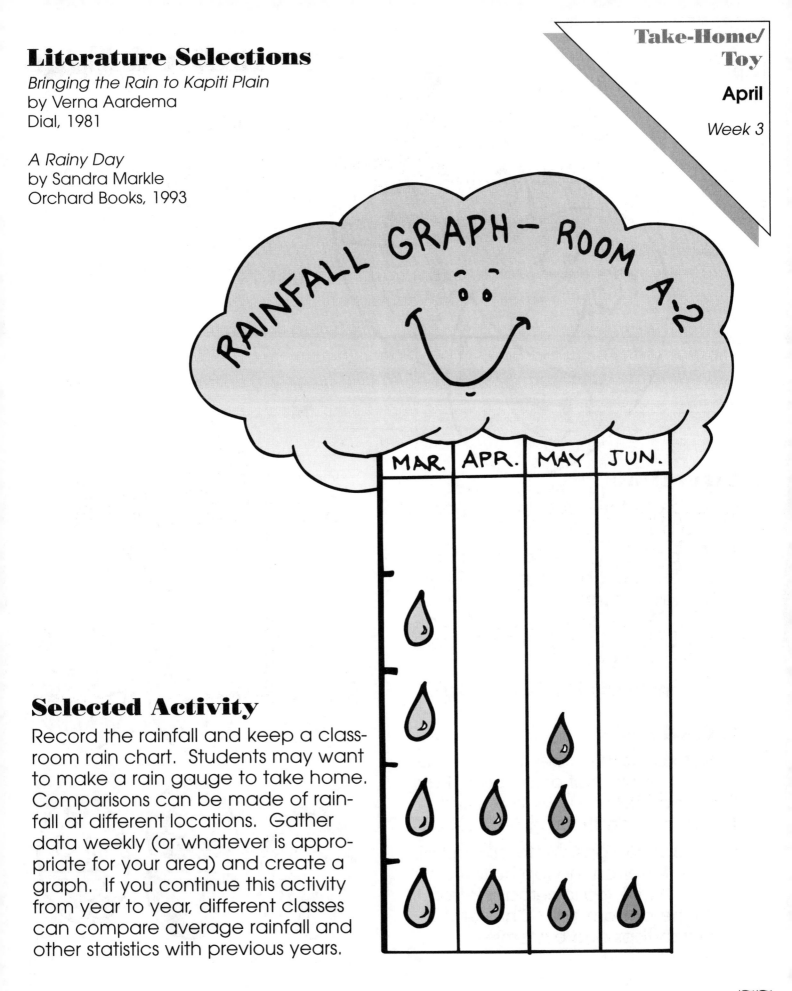

Selected Activity

Record the rainfall and keep a class-room rain chart. Students may want to make a rain gauge to take home. Comparisons can be made of rainfall at different locations. Gather data weekly (or whatever is appropriate for your area) and create a graph. If you continue this activity from year to year, different classes can compare average rainfall and other statistics with previous years.

Scrambled Eggs

Materials

plastic eggs (hosiery containers, Easter leftovers, etc.)

colored adhesive tape, yarn scraps, etc.

cardboard

markers

Directions

1. Separate the eggs into top halves and bottom halves.

2. Use colored adhesive tape to create eyes, eyebrows, noses, mustaches, etc., on the top halves of eggs. Make mouths, beards, collars, bow ties, etc., on the bottom halves of the eggs.

3. Mix and match the egg heads.

Variations

1. Write a math problem on the top and bottom half of the egg. Put the answer on a piece of cardboard inside the egg.

2. Collect 26 eggs. Write an uppercase letter on the top half of an egg. Write the lowercase letter on the bottom half. Children match tops and bottoms.

3. Ideas for pieces of cardboard to be placed inside each egg: scrambled spelling words, vocabulary words, color and matching color word, ABC order, numbers 1-100, etc.

Literature Selections

Chickens Aren't the Only Ones
by Ruth Heller
Grosset & Dunlap, 1981

Rechenka's Eggs
by Patricia Polacco
Philomel, 1988

Selected Activity

Store the eggs in a basket or
baskets. Label baskets by
category (spelling, math, letters,
etc.). Bring baskets out for an
extra treat or to be used when
children have finished their seat
work early.

Read-Treat: Cinco de Mayo Music Factory

Materials

two plastic laundry detergent scoops

two milk jug caps

aluminum pie tin

small pieces of plastic and pull tabs

gelatin boxes

sandpaper

one-liter plastic bottles

small plastic containers with lids

round cardboard oatmeal or cornmeal containers with lids

yarn

glue

tape

Directions

1. To make maracas, place some small pieces of cut-up plastic and a few soda pull tabs into the cup of a laundry detergent scoop. Glue on a second scoop. Let dry.

2. To make castanets, tape milk jug lids to thumb and forefinger.

3. To make a tambourine, tie pull tabs, soda caps and small pieces of cut-up plastic around the edge of an aluminum pie tin. Make sure the pieces of string or yarn are long enough for the object to strike the pie tin when shaken.

4. To make sand blocks, cut a piece of sandpaper the size of a gelatin box. Glue to the box. Rub two together.

5. To make shakers, add plastic pieces to small plastic containers. Attach lid and decorate.

6. To make a drum, decorate the outside of a round oatmeal or cornmeal container. Attach lid.

7. To make bottle horns, fill one-liter plastic bottles with varying amounts of water. Blow down into the bottle for an eerie sound.

Variations

Your recycling center will contain untold treasures to add to your music factory assembly line.

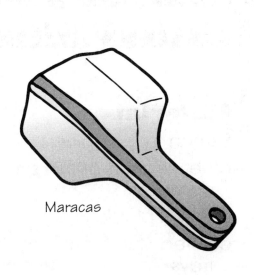

Maracas

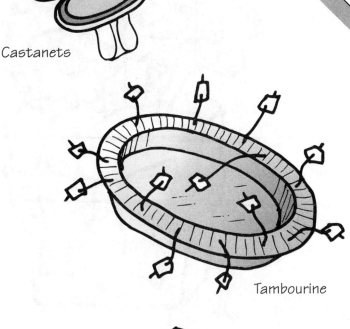

Castanets

Tambourine

Literature Selection

Cinco de Mayo
by Janet Riehecky
Children's, 1993

Selected Activity

The instruments from the music factory will lend just the right "tone" to your Cinco de Mayo celebration. You might want to create pinatas, large crepe paper flowers and other festive items to decorate your classroom. Consider inviting another class to join your celebration, or you might want to get permission to decorate a hallway or the school cafeteria.

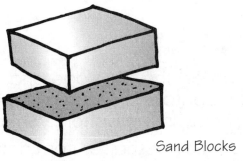

Sand Blocks

Shaker

Drum

Bottle Horn

Mother's Day Tussy Mussy

Materials

French fry containers

pipe cleaners or thin strips of cardboard

colored plastic jugs

colored Styrofoam™ meat trays

clay

plastic grocery bag cut into strips

Directions

1. Scallop the top edge of a French fry container. Place a small piece of clay in the bottom. Set aside.

2. Cut flower shapes from colored plastic jugs or from colored Styrofoam™ meat trays. Attach to pipe cleaners or cardboard stems.

3. Place stems into the clay in the bottom of the French fry container. Tie a plastic bag ribbon strip around the outside.

Literature Selection

The Mother's Day Mice
by Eve Bunting
Clarion, 1988

And Father's Day Tie

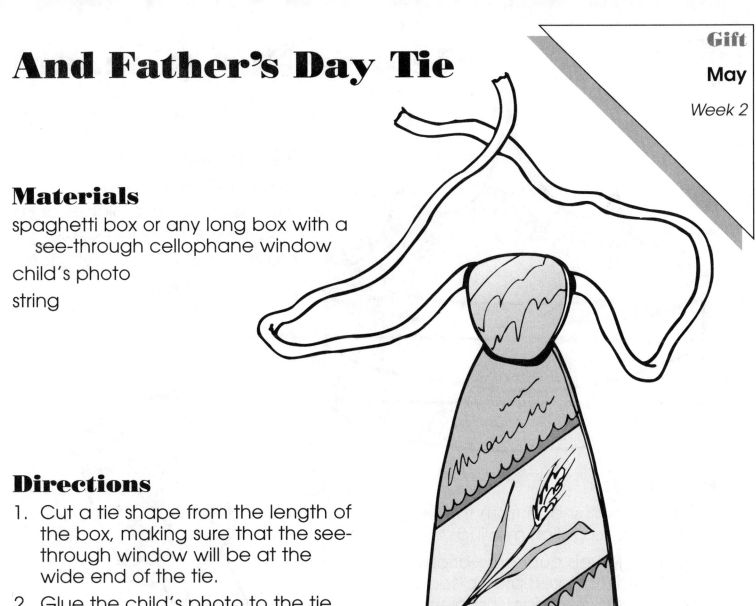

Materials

spaghetti box or any long box with a
  see-through cellophane window
child's photo
string

Directions

1. Cut a tie shape from the length of
   the box, making sure that the see-
   through window will be at the
   wide end of the tie.

2. Glue the child's photo to the tie
   so that it shows through the window. Trim photo if necessary.

3. Attach string to the knot-end of
   the tie so that Dad can wear it
   around his neck.

Variation

Create a "window" in any piece of
cardboard and cover with clear
plastic wrap.

Literature Selection

Your Dad Was Just Like You
by Dolores Johnson
Atheneum, 1993

Victoria Day (Canada)

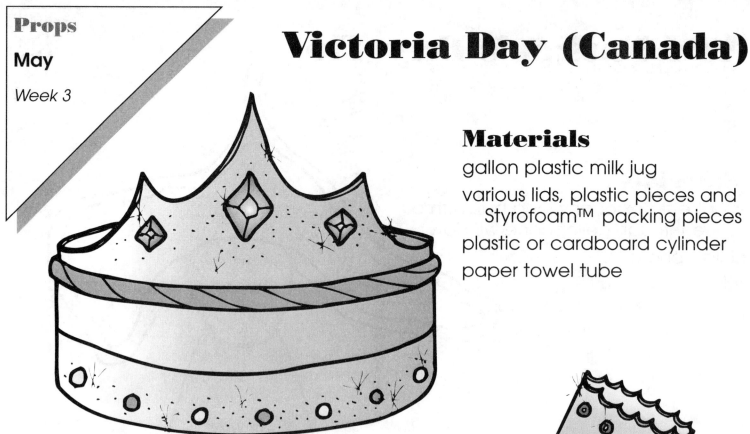

Materials

gallon plastic milk jug

various lids, plastic pieces and
   Styrofoam™ packing pieces

plastic or cardboard cylinder

paper towel tube

Directions

1. Cut a crown shape from the bottom of a gallon milk jug.

2. Glue on jewels cut from various plastic lids, colored plastic soda bottles or plastic packing pieces. See page 50 for suggestions.

3. Make a scepter from a plastic or cardboard cylinder. Scallop the top of the container, and glue on jewels cut from various pieces of plastic.

4. Glue a paper towel tube onto the bottom of the scepter.

Cut.

84

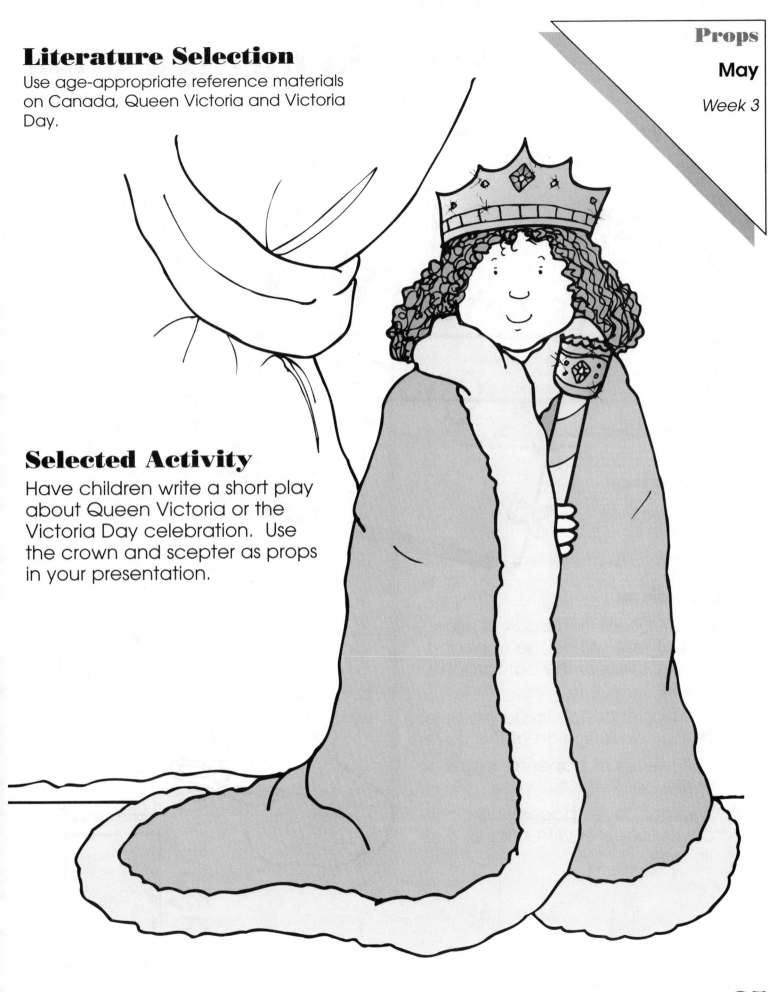

Literature Selection

Use age-appropriate reference materials on Canada, Queen Victoria and Victoria Day.

Selected Activity

Have children write a short play about Queen Victoria or the Victoria Day celebration. Use the crown and scepter as props in your presentation.

Autograph Book

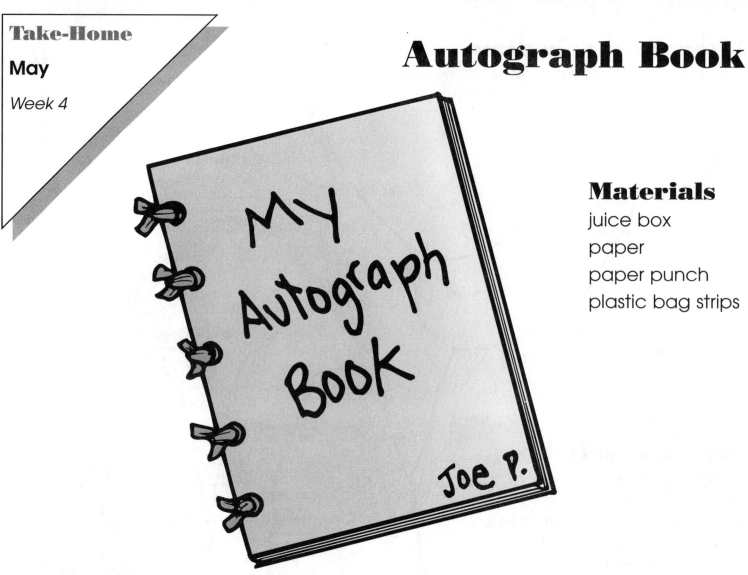

Materials

juice box
paper
paper punch
plastic bag strips

Directions

1. Cut out front and back of juice box. These will be the front and back covers of the autograph book.

2. Use paper punch to punch holes along one long side of the covers.

3. Cut pieces of paper for pages to fit the book.

4. Tie front cover, pages and back cover together with strips of plastic bag.

JUICE
BOX

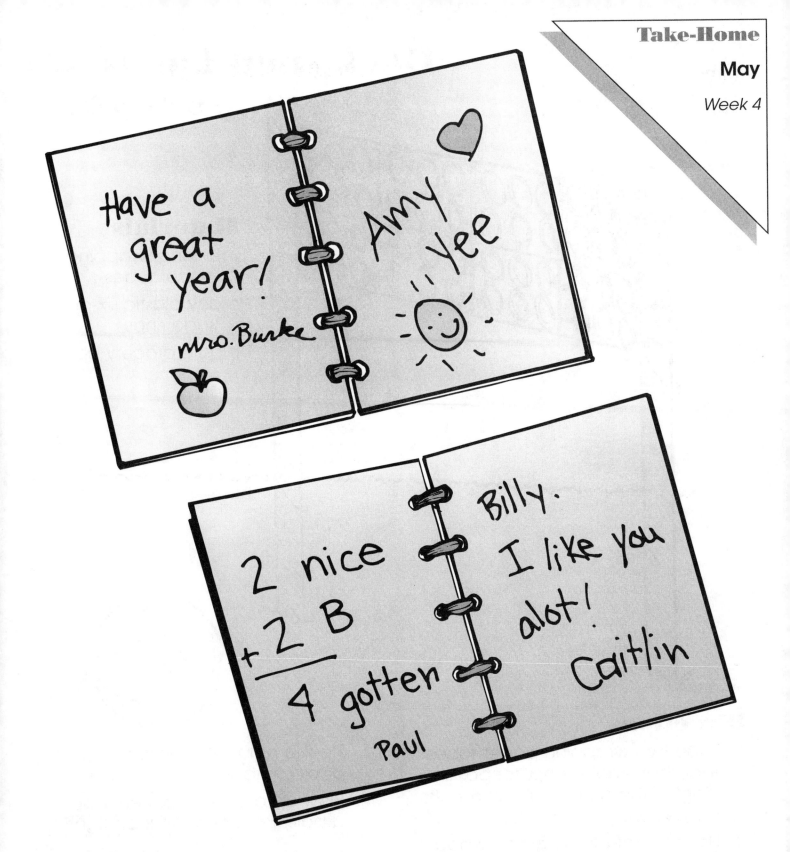

Literature Selection

Autographs! I Collect Them
by Margaret Frith
Random House, 1990

Selected Activity

It's fun to collect and exchange photographs, phone numbers and friendly messages with classmates as the school year comes to an end.

Backyard Carnival: Volleyball

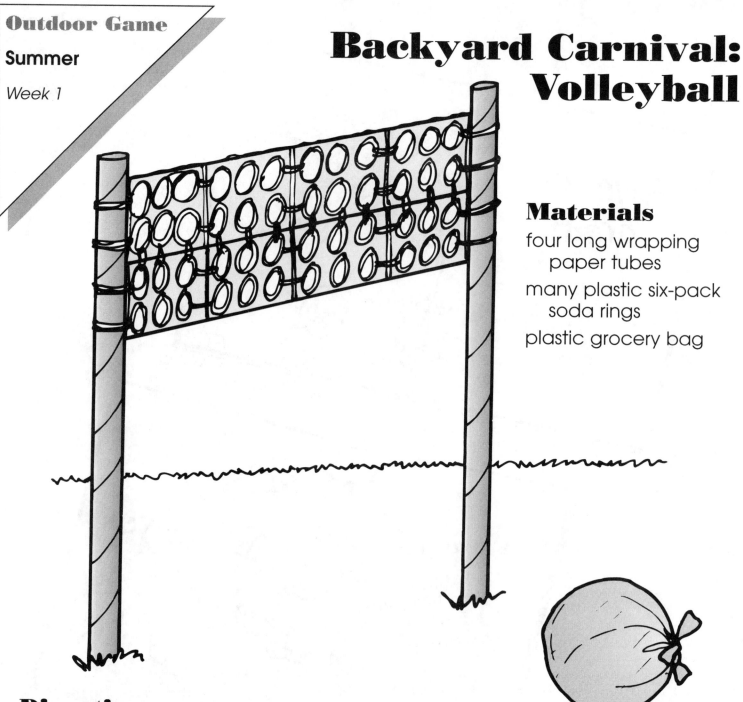

Materials

four long wrapping
   paper tubes

many plastic six-pack
   soda rings

plastic grocery bag

Directions

1. Tape two wrapping paper tubes together, end to end, for posts. Plant in the ground about 6' (1.8 cm) apart.

2. Use strips of plastic grocery bag to tie the six-pack plastic rings together. You'll need to create a net that is about 6' (1.8 cm) long and two or three six-pack ring forms deep.

3. Tie the net to the posts with strips of plastic bag.

4. Blow up a plastic grocery bag for a ball. Be sure to tie it off tightly.

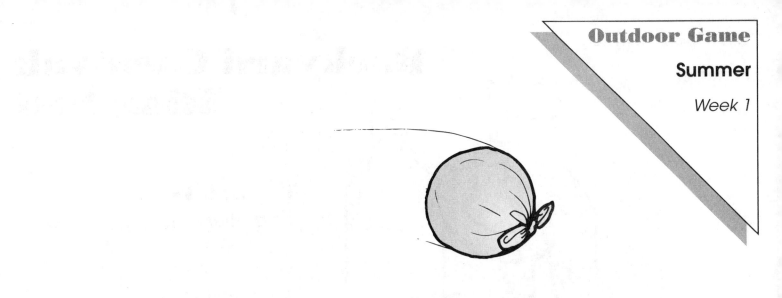

Literature Selection

The Silver Sports Series
by Carol Nicklaus
Silver Press, 1991

Selected Activities

Turn your volleyball game into an instant math activity. Assign students to keep score, record the total number of hits, number of hits per player, number of misses, etc.

You can adapt the volleyball game to fit other subject areas, too. For example, a player serving the ball might call out the name of a state. In order to return the volley, a player might have to name that state's capital.

Note

Adjust the length of your net to fit your playing space.

Backyard Carnival: Ring Toss

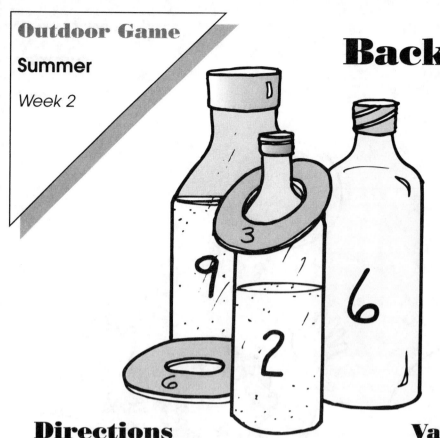

Materials

tall bottles of various shapes and sizes

sand or gravel

adhesive labels

marker

Styrofoam™ meat trays, cereal boxes or plastic detergent bottles

Directions

1. Fill tall bottles with a little sand or gravel to make them steadier.

2. Arrange tall bottles in a row.

3. Assign a point value to each bottle, and write the number on an adhesive label. Affix label to the front of the bottle.

4. Make various sizes of rings. Cut circles from Styrofoam™ meat trays or cereal boxes. You can also make rings from plastic soda bottles.

5. Assign a point value to each ring, and write the number on an adhesive label. Affix label to the ring.

6. Children take turns tossing the rings at the bottles from a predetermined distance. When a ring lands on a bottle, add the point values and keep score.

Variations

1. Make the center holes of the rings different sizes. The smaller the hole, the higher the point value.

2. Once children seem to have mastered tossing the rings over the bottles, increase the distance from which the rings are thrown.

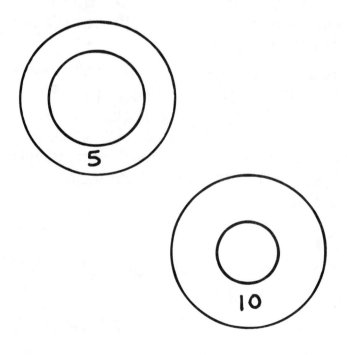

Literature Selection

Game for a Game?
by Robynne Eagan
Teaching & Learning Company, 1995

Selected Activity

Instead of point values, you can write vocabulary words or math problems or other curriculum topics on the bottles. When a ring lands on a bottle, the child must respond correctly in order to score.

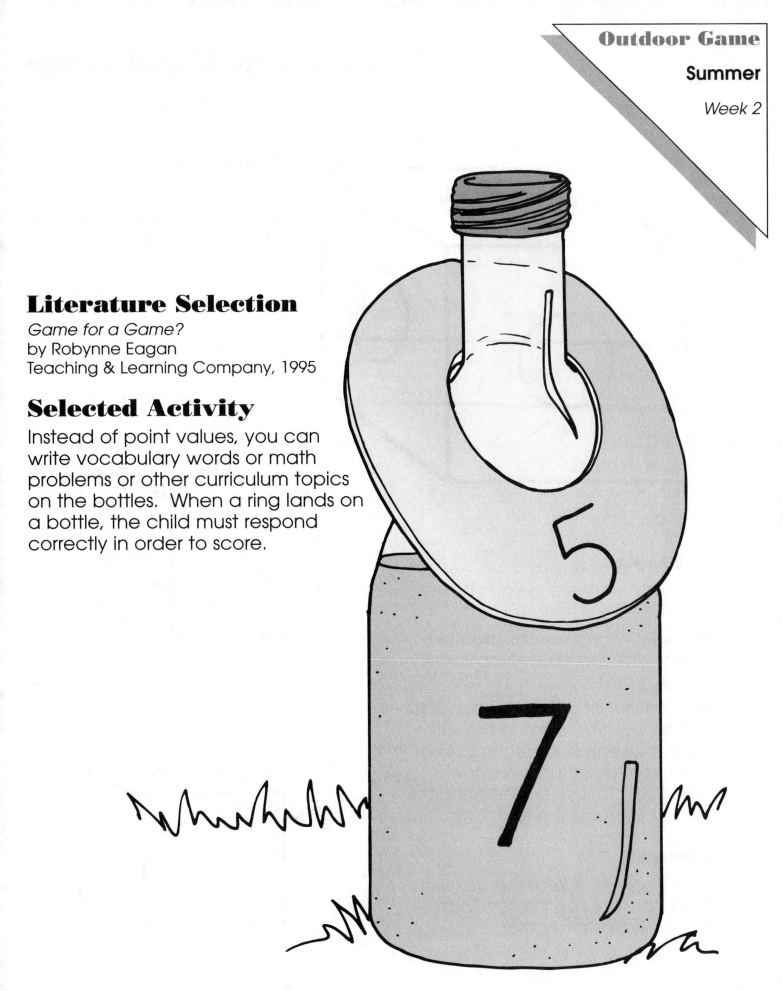

Roll-a-Color

Materials

three gelatin boxes
scrap or construction paper
colored markers
glue

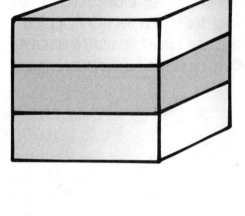

Directions

1. Tape or glue three gelatin boxes together.

2. Wrap with scrap or construction paper. Tape or glue the paper in place.

3. Make a dot of color on each side of the box. You can do this with marker, or you can cut a circle of color from construction paper and glue on. Use a different color for each side of the box.

Variation

Cover the entire side of the box with colored construction paper. Make each side a different color.

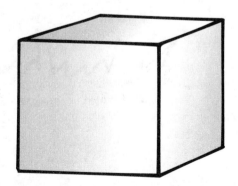

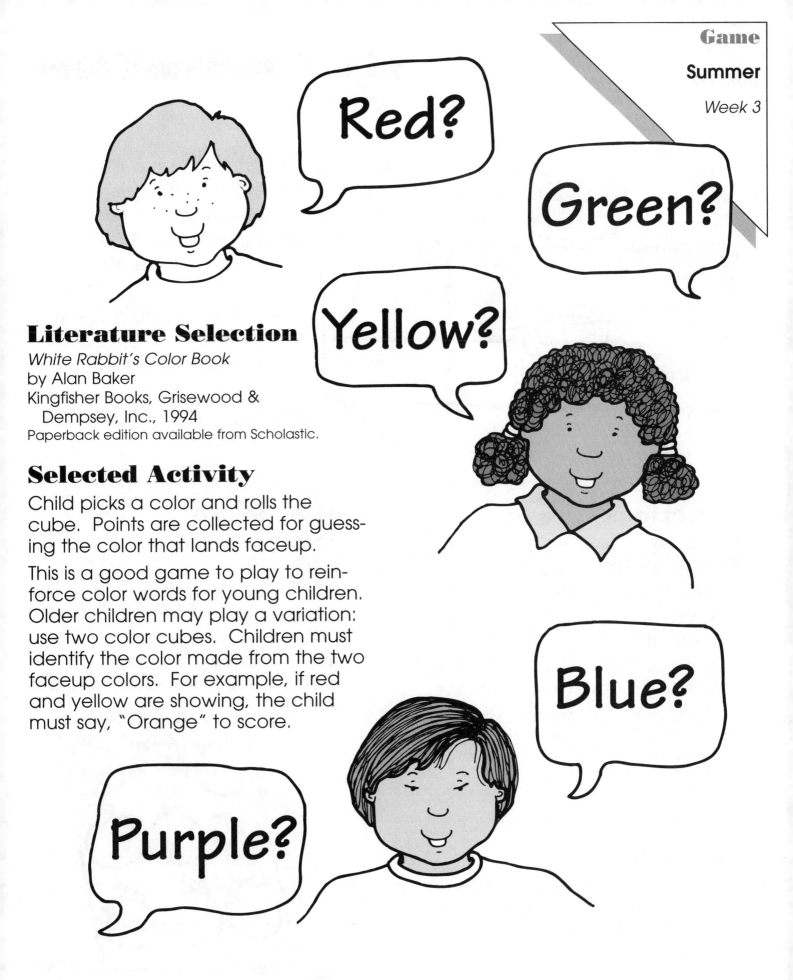

Red?

Green?

Yellow?

Literature Selection

White Rabbit's Color Book
by Alan Baker
Kingfisher Books, Grisewood &
   Dempsey, Inc., 1994
Paperback edition available from Scholastic.

Selected Activity

Child picks a color and rolls the cube. Points are collected for guessing the color that lands faceup.

This is a good game to play to reinforce color words for young children. Older children may play a variation: use two color cubes. Children must identify the color made from the two faceup colors. For example, if red and yellow are showing, the child must say, "Orange" to score.

Blue?

Purple?

Lid Toss and More

Materials

10 flat plastic milk lids

indelible marker

five or more butter tubs or
other deli containers

nine or more plastic grocery
bags

large cardboard

tape

small zipper plastic bags filled
with beans or rice

Directions
Lid Toss

1. Write a point value on each milk
   lid with indelible marker.

2. Write a number (1-5) on each of
   the butter tubs.

3. Children toss a milk lid into a tub
   from a predetermined distance.

4. Add/multiply/subtract/divide the
   numbers. Score points for correct
   answers.

Balloon Board

1. Inflate grocery bags and tie off
   tightly.

2. Prop up cardboard against a wall
   or table. Tape inflated grocery
   bags to the board.

3. Throw beanbag at balloons. A hit
   scores a point. Replace deflated
   bags for the next player.

94

Materials

Styrofoam™ meat trays
plastic baby pool
plastic bottle
dowel rod or stick
string

10 one-liter plastic bottles
used aluminum foil

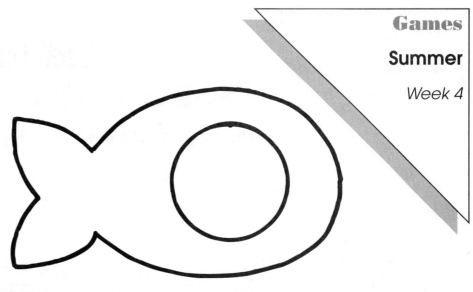

Bowling

1. Collect 10 one-liter bottles, number them 1-10 and arrange bowling-pin-style.

2. Crumple up enough aluminum foil to make a sizeable bowling ball.

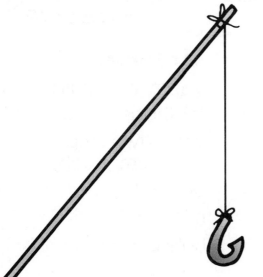

Fishing Pond

1. Fill baby pool with water.

2. Cut fish from Styrofoam™ meat trays. Cut out extra large eye-holes (so children can easily "hook" the fish). Place fish in baby pool.

3. Attach string to dowel rod or stick.

4. Cut a hook from a plastic bottle. Attach hook to end of string.

5. Go fish! (You can assign point values to the fish; write them on with marker.)

Literature Selection

The Carnival in My Mind
by Barbara Wersba
HarperCollins, 1982

Happy Birthday: Bubble Blower Necklace, Book Cover and Spiral Toy

Materials

35mm film container with lid

toothpaste cap

string (two lengths, about 20" (51 cm) each)

glue

milk jug

hole punch

Directions
Bubble Blower Necklace

1. Glue toothpaste cap to lid of film container. Let dry.

2. Glue necklace-length string to either side of film container. Let dry.

3. Cut out a bubble blower from a milk jug. See illustration.

4. Punch a hole in the end of the handle and thread through neck-lace-length string.

5. Fill film container with bubble solution.

Variations

Cut different shapes for bubble blowers from plastic bottles. Try an oval, star, triangle, etc.

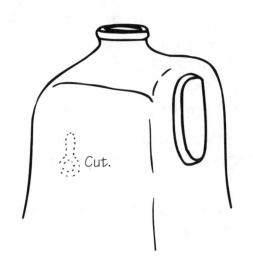

Cut.

Materials

cardboard

fabric strips or rickrack

stickers, stamps, buttons, glitter, etc.

plastic soda bottle

Spiral Toy

1. Cut off tip and bottom of plastic soda bottle.
2. Draw a continuous line around the outside of the bottle. The line should be spaced about $1/2$" (1.25 cm).
3. Cut bottle along the line.

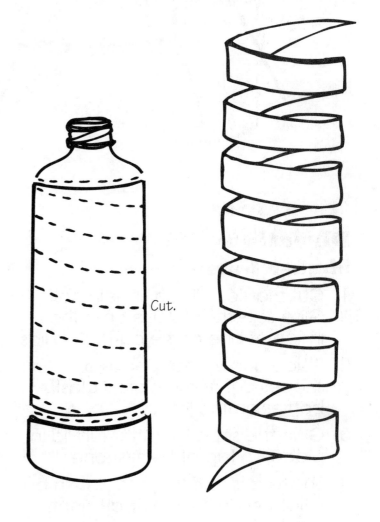

Cut.

Book Cover

1. Measure cardboard so that it is as tall as the book you wish to cover and about 6" (15 cm) longer.
2. Fold cardboard in half, length-wise.
3. Cut out handles on either side. Handles can be about 2" (5 cm) tall. Refold cardboard around the book, this time allowing for the book's spine.
4. Decorate the outside of the book cover with fabric, rickrack, glitter, stickers, stamps, etc.

Get Well Games

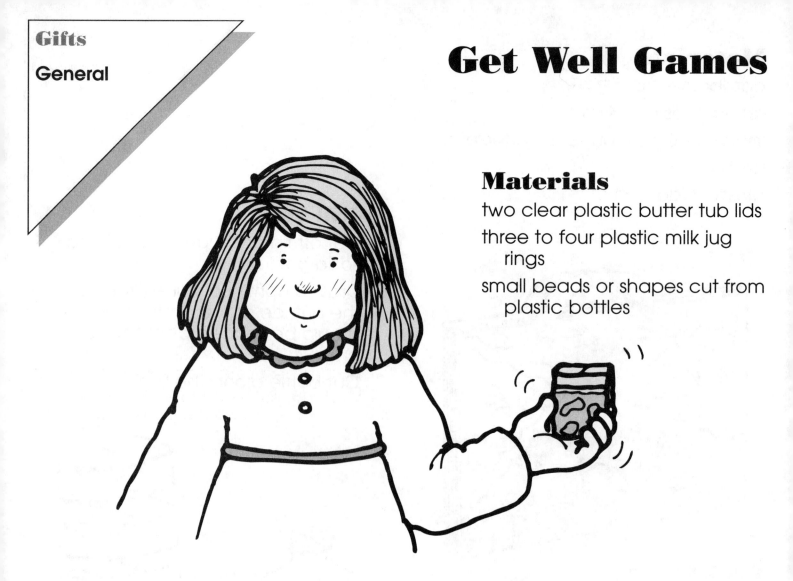

Materials
two clear plastic butter tub lids

three to four plastic milk jug
rings

small beads or shapes cut from
plastic bottles

Directions
Shaker Game

1. Cut plastic milk jug rings in half.
   Glue several in place onto the
   inside of one of the butter tub lids.

2. Place a few small beads or
   shapes cut from colored plastic
   bottles on the lid.

3. Glue the second butter tub lid in
   place on top of the first one.

4. Shake to see if the beads can be
   captured in the compartments
   made by the ring halves.

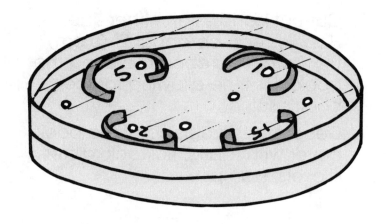

Materials

plastic breath mint boxes
cooking oil
food coloring
small plastic zipper bag
$1/2$ cup (120 ml) ketchup

Almost Magic Slate

1. Add $1/2$ cup (120 ml) ketchup in plastic bag and zip closed. Make sure the seal is complete!

2. Lay flat and smooth out ketchup.

3. Draw pictures with your finger; erase by smoothing out ketchup with the palm of your hand.

Oil and Water Game

1. Fill plastic breath mint box almost to the top with water. Add a few drops of food coloring, and shake to mix.

2. Add $1/2$ teaspoon (2.5 ml) of cooking oil.

3. Shake!

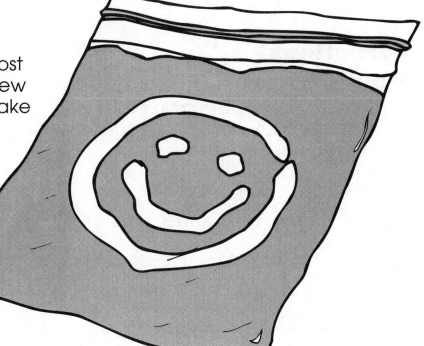

Good-Bye and Hello Gifts

Materials

plastic breath mint boxes

children's school pictures or other individual portraits

Directions
Good-Bye Gift

1. Give each child a plastic breath mint box. Have children place their school pictures inside the box, or draw a picture of themselves to fit inside.

2. Glue the boxes together.

Note

This not only makes a nice gift to give a departing student but also an appropriate one for a principal, student teacher, cook, janitor or other staff member who is leaving.

100

Materials

glue
colorful paper scraps
cereal box
hole punch
yarn

Welcome Gift

1. Cut away the top, bottom and both long sides from a cereal box. The remaining pieces will be the front and back covers of your book.

2. Wrap the covers in colorful paper scraps. Cut letters from large headlines to make the title for your book. Glue in place on the front cover.

3. Create pages for the inside of your book. Each student may wish to contribute a page about himself or draw a picture. You may also wish to include schedules, a calendar of special events, classroom rules, etc. Don't forget the title page, where contributors, authors and artists are credited.

4. Hole-punch the left side of your front cover and pages and the right side of the back cover. Assemble the book and bind with yarn.

Note

This not only makes a nice gift to give an arriving student but also an appropriate one for a new principal, student teacher, cook, janitor or other staff member.

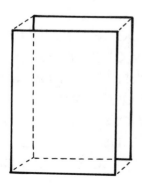

Congratulations!

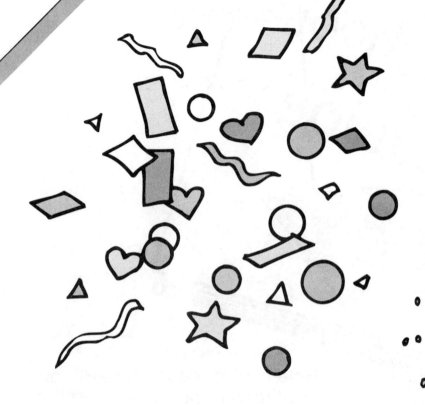

Materials
colored plastic soda bottles
cereal boxes
old greeting cards
other colorful paper scraps

Directions
1. Cut any of the above listed material into small, pleasing shapes.
2. Gather together for a special event, and celebrate with your colorful confetti.

Note
There are paper punches available in a variety of shapes. You may have or wish to borrow some of these to make some of your confetti shapes. *These punches were created for use with paper only–do not use on plastic soda bottles.*

102